THE
THREE
BOOKS OF BUSINESS

An insightful and concise guide to improve
the Customer Service Representative, Sales
Professional, and Manager within you!

By Roger Reynold

Featuring:

The Handbook of Service for Good Business

The Handbook of Sales for More Business

The Handbook of Management for Better Business

About the Author

Roger Reynold has spent over half his business career in the Fortune 100 Realm, with over 27 years in the transportation industry. The first nine years were in customer service where he won numerous awards, including The Customer Satisfaction Award in Fiscal Year (FY) 1996, a select accolade given to those providing outstanding customer service. He attained International Customer Service Representative of the Year in FY '95. Awards followed his years in Field Sales, including Account Executive of the Year for his Region in FY 2001, AE Supplier of the Year given by one of his largest customers in 2004, and President's Club in FY 2008. Roger also has management experience in the newspaper industry and supervisory experience in the health club field.

General Introduction

Roger attributes much of his business accomplishments to the skills he developed in customer service. He believes a service approach should be incorporated into whatever position is held within a company. Add a people-oriented mindset to this and success can then follow in the careers of Customer Service, Sales, and Management.

Roger began writing this book while going through cancer treatment in 2002, when he later received a clean bill of health. A strong desire to give more back came to him and the intentions of this book are to improve readers' performance and make the business world a more positive place. This book was completed years later and refined since then, giving it the advantage of further business experience.

The Handbook of Service for Good Business, The Handbook of Sales for More Business, and *The Handbook of Management for Better Business* contain valuable insights and concepts. The books can bring new dimensions to any skill set, and bring about positive changes for not only the employee, but also to his/her internal customers (within the company) and external customers. It truly is an inspirational and informative guide. The first book is the most technical of the three, and the following two are an easier read. The Handbooks are written in a concise format so that all of the writings can be useful and informative. One of the chapters from the Customer Service Handbook is repeated in the Sales Handbook and one is repeated in the Management Handbook because the chapters also apply directly to those fields.

Regardless of the exact profession you are in or pursuing, Roger hopes you will take the time to read all three Handbooks. Knowledge in one area will help gain proficiency in another. Anyone dealing with people in their profession should benefit from all three handbooks.

There are also two Afterword's following the Three Books touching on success in the business world, and balancing of the consumer, profit and free market. These are a must read.

Please note the buyers and readers of <u>The Three Books of Business</u> assume responsibility for implementing any of the book's concepts/material, and the outcomes from these implementations.

Master Table of Contents

Book I – The Handbook of Service for Good Business

Dedication 5

Introduction 7

Chapter 1) The Ultimate Customer 9

Chapter 2) The K's & P's of Customer Service 13

Chapter 3) You Can Handle It! 19

Chapter 4) One Call at a Time 21

Chapter 5) Agent Empowerment 25

Chapter 6) Customer Empowerment 29

Chapter 7) Think Internal, not only External! 33

Chapter 8) Employee versus Contractor?

     The Results should be the same! 35

Chapter 9) Face-to-Face Service 37

Chapter 10) Selling in the Service Call..............................41

Chapter 11) Oh Sales...Don't Forget the Service!......................45

Chapter 12) Notes to Management 49

Chapter 13) An Attitude of Service..53

Book II – The Handbook of Sales for More Business

Dedication..61

Introduction 63

Chapter 1) Attributes of Successful Sales Professionals.............65

Chapter 2) Relationship Building 71

Chapter 3) Don't Forget the Service!..................................75

Chapter 4) Persistence, Rejection, Performance............................79

Chapter 5) Bring Your Own Personality 83

Chapter 6) Retaining instead of Neglecting....................................87

Chapter 7) Grow the Business...91

Chapter 8) Keep it Simple 95

Chapter 9) Seniors, help the Juniors...99

Book III – The Handbook of Management for Better Business

Dedication... 107

Introduction 109

Chapter 1) Attributes of Successful Managers 111

Chapter 2) Building the Manager Employee Relationship 115

Chapter 3) Management Integrity 119

Chapter 4) Service Your Employees............................... 123

Chapter 5) Coach and Trainer.. 127

Chapter 6) The Natural Manager &

    the Called to Management........................... 131

Chapter 7) Managing a Labor Intensive Work Force 135

Chapter 8) Managing the Sales Professional 139

Chapter 9) Managing the Manager................................... 143

Chapter 10) Setting the Course...................................... 147

Chapter 11) Notes to Management 151

-Afterword I-

What is Success in Business?

-Afterword II-

The Ultimate Customer, Profit, and the Free Market

Thank you to the Reader

References

Book I

<u>The Handbook of Service for Good Business</u>

Roger Reynold

Copyright 2010

Table of Contents

Book I – The Handbook of Service for Good Business

Dedication 5

Introduction 7

Chapter 1) The Ultimate Customer 9

Chapter 2) The K's & P's of Customer Service.................. 13

Chapter 3) You Can Handle It! 19

Chapter 4) One Call at a Time 21

Chapter 5) Agent Empowerment 25

Chapter 6) Customer Empowerment 29

Chapter 7) Think Internal, not only External!..................... 33

Chapter 8) Employee versus Contractor?

                 The Results should be the same!........................ 35

Chapter 9) Face-to-Face Service 37

Chapter 10) Selling in the Service Call....................................41

Chapter 11) Oh Sales...Don't Forget the Service!..............47

Chapter 12) Notes to Management...49

Chapter 13) An Attitude of Service..53

Dedication

This "Handbook" is for all the Customer Service Representatives who perform their duties with a sincere desire to help their customers. It is also for all sales professionals and managers, who incorporate customer service into their positions and in so doing, make their companies a better place. Finally, it is for all of you who read this book and wish to improve your own customer service skill set.

Introduction to Book One

This book will provide an understanding of the importance of customer service in the business world at <u>all</u> levels, help you to learn "An Attitude of Service," and reveal the fruits this attitude brings.

Customer Service is no longer solely a department within a business, but rather a must-have attribute of every employee. In today's age, the wants and needs of both internal and external customers are so high they require every individual to gain a service mind-set. Whether you're a customer service representative, a sales professional on the road, someone who finds himself in top management or the owner of a business, true success requires you to find and hone the customer service within you.

This book will help you achieve this, and improve its effectiveness.

Chapter 1

The Ultimate Customer

Excellent customer service must first start with an understanding of who your "ultimate customers" are. The mission statement of your firm can be a good indicator. A simpler way is to determine who out there in John Q. Public is ultimately paying your salary.

Customer Service Representatives (Agents) usually have a good understanding of who the Ultimate Customers are and what they need because Customer Service Reps interface with them daily. However, it is a good idea for all employees to remember who eventually is behind their paychecks – customers whose needs have been met. It is so easy for an employee who is removed from external customer contact to forget the value his or her work brings to the outside world. Do the employees in maintenance realize the importance of their work, and how their efforts give the necessary environment for Ms. Sales to close the deal or Mr. Customer Representative to service new and existing customers? Realizing the value of what you do brings higher self respect, and higher productivity.

Note to management – Make sure everyone in the company realizes the importance of what they do, and how it eventually affects the customer.

Your Ultimate Customers are in one of three categories:

1.) End Users

2.) Those in a specific Target Market

3.) Customers in Various Markets

End Users

Many industries' Ultimate Customers are the final users of the product or service. The toy store owner sells toys to children and their parents. Any customer service follow-up in exchanges/returns/complaints are done specifically with these customers and no other parties. The Pet Grooming Facility services the pet and has customer contact with the owner. Again, this is more of a direct customer relationship where the service provided pertains to an end user. Ultimate Customers falling in the End User category are in a simple and direct relationship. The customer service contact between the business and customer only involves these two interested parties.

Those in a Specific Target Market

Many industries have a specific target market where their ultimate customers will be found. The Injection Molding Machine Corporation you may work for has five main clients for whom they supply machines and parts. These five customers are this corporation's Ultimate Customers. Each of the five customers may have specific needs they are looking for from your firm. Although all five may be in a similar industry, keep in mind each one of these five Companies has their own Ultimate Customer Base they are selling to and servicing. You may never have contact with these companies directly, but they may hear about your firm if your customers' ultimate customers do not feel satisfied. When your Ultimate Customers call you up for assistance, they have their own customers' expectations they are trying to meet and exceed. At times, their needs may seem elevated based on their own customer expectations. Ultimate Customers in the same target market will have many similarities in the service relationship with your company, but keep in mind there may be differences as well, and customer individualism must be considered.

Customers in Various Markets

Your industry may require you to service companies in various markets. The Hotel Industry serves individuals, corporations, clubs and outings. The customer service representative of a large dot com firm may talk to a grandmother ordering a sweater for her daughter, and the next call may be with a V.P. of a Fortune 500 Company submitting a 300 piece bulk order. The customer service rep quickly learns the needs of each Ultimate Customer can vary.

What should the common goal be of servicing the three kinds of Ultimate Customers? TOTAL CUSTOMER FULFILLMENT: I know, I know, easier said than done. I think The K's & P's of Customer Service can help.

Chapter 2

The K's & P's of Customer Service

The Bar has been raised, and you're actually going to attempt total satisfaction over the phone or in person. Relying on your own "K's & P's" will help:

1.) Knowledge of your Customers

2.) Knowledge of the Product

3.) Professionalism

4.) Positive Approach

Taking customer calls for a living can be one of the most challenging endeavors. At the same time, it can be very rewarding and develop skills within you that can be applied to future careers. I know many people who have decided on a career in customer service and wish to keep directly interfacing with customers daily. These people are abundant in the Two K's & P's. Get to know them personally whenever possible. They are a wealth of knowledge and are invaluable in the advice department. Hearing about their experiences can help you with future problem calls. Now, getting back to the K's and P's.

Knowledge of Your Customer

Knowing who your "Ultimate Customers" are and which category they fall into is a great start. This will give the Customer Service Representative a basis from which to start interfacing with his or her customers. Truly knowing your customers will still come from job experience. By the sheer number of calls that will come in, the Customer Service Representative quickly gains a general idea of what many of the UC's needs are and how to satisfy them. The customer rep may speak to a different client on every call, but usually some customer needs become more prevalent than others. A majority may start to become routine, but you will still have plenty of calls ahead to keep your job interesting!

Your industry may provide you the opportunity to only deal with certain customers on a daily basis. A setting like this allows more of a personal relationship to develop between you and the consumer. The customer knows you will be on the other end of the phone when he calls, and consulting usually takes place as an additional venue. This can be a very fortunate setting for customer agents who want to provide more tailor-made solutions to problems, and have a professional personal relationship with their clients (similar to sales).

I believe Customer Representatives learn what makes their UC's tick as much as anyone else. They speak to a Corporation's customer base daily, handle routine requests, and are also the first ones to address a "customer crisis." Every call a representative takes is an opportunity to make your company shine. It is a professional responsibility, and carries more weight than many realize.

Knowledge of the Product

Knowledge of your firm's product or service should be included in your corporate training.

Note to management – Training Customer Reps so that they are familiar with your companies' products should be fully covered in C.S. training. Also, regular training throughout the year on current and new products is highly recommended.

Customers are so impressed when they call a company and the Customer Rep has an excellent understanding of the product. Customers love "One Stop Shopping" whenever possible, and hope to avoid a transfer. Know the products and services in your department, and the customer will develop respect for you. A good friend of mine who recently retired from field sales took a part time job at a hardware store. Full training was promised to him, but as they were short handed he was given a two-hour cram session on saws. He was then given the responsibility of managing the entire saw department. Throughout the day, various customers came to him asking him questions he could not answer. At 3:00 pm he thanked management for the offer, but told them the customer service within him would not allow him to give only half-baked answers to these customers, and he needed more training.

Professionalism and Staying Positive

These words are used frequently in today's business world. Be Professional, or Stay Positive, is heard from management and coworkers in every department. A unique challenge faced white collar professionals during the Depression, but stress may be even more prevalent in today's business world. Challenges are facing employees and corporations at an accelerated rate.

The Customer Service Representative (CSR) who is "Professional" and maintains a "Positive Mental Attitude" really stands out.   Problem calls and upset customers are part of the job. At times, it is necessary for the customer service knowledge you have within to remind you of professional basics during the call:

    a. Utilize professional greetings such as "Mr." or "Miss" when appropriate.

    b. Show an understanding of the customer's plight:"I'm sorry to hear that and I understand how you feel, Mr. Customer, let me see what I can do for you right now."

    c. If you cannot solve the problem directly, determine the course of action that will.

    d. Keep a smile in your tone of voice.

    e. Allow the customer to vent when needed, then...

    f. Take control of the call.

Most successful managers in the workplace have one trait in common; they always remain positive about the problem and never make it personal. Customer Service Agents need to do the same thing and take control of the call using the aforementioned tips. The following chapter will elaborate further.

Chapter 3

You Can Handle It!

Customer – I think I'm going to need a manager.

CSR – I can get a manager for you, but I have been a Customer Representative for quite a while, may I help you?

Customer – The last two agents couldn't, and you think you can??

CSR – I would sure like to try, and if I can't I will find someone who can. What is the problem you are going through?

This was an actual customer service dialogue. The outcome was the customer allowed the agent to help her, and requesting a manager was not necessary. A majority of customers will allow you to assist them in scenarios similar to these. Customers who sense a sincere desire to help and competence at the other end of the phone will usually allow the rep to solve the problem and avoid a manager transfer.

Note to management – Recognize the Customer Representatives who have done their job over time and done it well. Awards and promotions within customer service give the agent something to strive for, and increases morale. This practice can also reduce Manager Transfer calls.

Utilizing the K's and P's can apply to both irritated and regular callers. The Customer Representative may also have to do a quick role reversal and put themselves in the place of the caller. If I had experienced what the customer has, would I be calling this disappointed?? Is there any similar experience I have had where I actually played this role

Dissatisfied callers are definitely the most challenging, but they also provide a great opportunity for you and your company to stand out. Engaging the K's and P's along with solving the customers' dilemmas can leave a good taste in their mouths, even if they feel your company caused this problem to begin with. Deep down the customer is still looking for empathy to their situation and for someone who is really concerned. A customer, who finds an agent that displays these traits, may then allow the agent to help him. Genuine concern toward the customers' plights will still leave them in a better state after they hang up, even if the dilemma is not totally resolved.

Chapter 4

One Call at a Time

I previously mentioned that taking customer calls can be one of the most challenging endeavors. Aside from an upset customer calling, an agent must also face and be prepared for the sheer number of daily calls that can be received. Guidelines your reps can follow are in M.P.U.B.

1.) Mentally Prepare

2.) Pace Yourself

3.) Utilize Breaks, Lunches, Activities

4.) Back Up Plan

Mentally Prepare

Most days the CSR will come to work ready for the job. The agent will come to know what to expect and his or her confidence level will grow with time. There are days however when a rep can be inundated with problem calls. It is hard to go home with a positive attitude on days like this. The CSR must utilize home time to relax and get away from the job. Occupy yourself with activities that take your mind off work. Use this time to be able to come back the next business day with a clear mind. Mentally prepare yourself by recognizing there may be some problem calls waiting, but probably not in the numbers that came in yesterday. Needlepoint, reading, light music (if allowed) between calls or at home can calm many a storm. Meditation and daily prayers have worked for centuries in combating daily stress.

Pace Yourself

Never sound rushed over the phone because it makes customers feel you want to get off the phone with them. You may be taking too many calls if you sound rushed. A repetitive job such as customer service requires you to get into a pace which will sound professional and positive to the customer and is still efficient for your company.

Utilize Breaks/Lunches/Assignments

These times can be enhanced by activities and mindsets found in "Mental Preparation" and "Pacing Yourself." Take advantage of your breaks and lunches so you can come back to the job with a relaxed focus. Many people find value in taking brisk walks during their breaks, getting out of the building, or spending time talking to fellow coworkers during lunch. These are all great ways to "unwind" and be ready for the next set of customer calls. Guard against getting into complaint sessions with your coworkers as this will produce a negative energy.

Productive Activities are a great way to broaden your horizons when call volume is low. Perhaps management will have you help with special projects. Take advantage of these opportunities whenever possible as it will broaden your horizons and could lead to a new career challenge.

Back-Up Plan

Arrange a back-up plan with your manager, one you may use when needed after intense calls. The most common is to sign out for a minute or two and regroup. This should never be abused and only used when necessary.

Note to management – Recognize the need for MPUB and help your CSRs in any area needed. You may have different suggestions for each individual to help them deal with the day-to-day stress of customer service.

Proper preparation in all of the aforementioned is a proactive approach that can empower you to overcome future obstacles.

Chapter 5

Agent Empowerment

To so many customers, the Customer Service Agent is the Company they're doing business with. Depending on the business, the CSA may be the only person the customer interfaces with and does not have a need or opportunity to see field sales or speak to inside sales over the phone. The Customer Service Representative in these cases is solely representing his/her company. Many times the customer does speak to sales, but still talks to the CSA more frequently.

The responsibility a Customer Service Representative holds is higher than many understand. There have been cases where a Corporation may pull its business because of a conversation it had with Customer Service. There have been many cases where Corporations give more business to a firm because of their customer service.

Note to Management – Make sure the Customer Service Representatives understand they are truly "representing" their entire company, just as sales professionals do in the field. Their actions can affect the bottom line as much as revenue generating departments.

There are three kinds of Caller/Customer Service Representative relationships:

1.) Rotating

2.) Virtual

3.) Selected

Rotating

The personal relationship a rep has with the customer grows with each kind of call. Rotating is when calls come into Customer Service at random, and are distributed to agents on a rotating basis. If there are not a lot of reps in the call center, agents may start to develop a relationship with customers based on how much they call and how often the customer obtains a certain representative.

Virtual

Virtual adds a little more personal touch. In these cases, the calls are still coming in on a rotating basis, however technology brings up a file on the customer so the agent knows whom they're speaking to before the customer says one word. They may also see a snapshot of the company's last interface with the customer so the rep may even know why the party is calling.

Selected

Finally, Selected refers to customers being able to obtain a certain representative or select group of representatives. In these cases the agent truly develops a personal relationship with the customer, paralleling sales. The agent may remember a few of the customer's personal traits and touch on them during the call.

"So how is your golf game going, Mr. Jones? The last I remember you were just about to break 80, right?"

Companies may also deploy a combination of the above. Customers usually prefer to develop a relationship with customer reps and love to get the same people they have confidence in or had good experiences with. In today's market, the Customer Service Agent is doing more than giving information or directing the calls to the proper departments. The CSA is truly becoming a problem solver and consultant.

It is up to the Corporation to set guidelines on the realm of the CSR's duties and responsibilities. Agent empowerment is prevalent today. As corporations grow, it is necessary to empower agents so the customers' needs are addressed as quickly as is possible and not make the customer always go through channels. Today, customer reps in many companies are empowered to do various tasks for the customer that before had to go through the billing, claims, or other departments. Corporations are relying on the good judgment and "professionalism" of the agent in these customer interfaces so the customer's needs are met sooner and satisfaction is reinforced. Can anyone think of a more important position?

Chapter 6

Customer Empowerment

For the first time in the history of business, technology is allowing the customer to perform many of the duties which previously could only be done by customer service. Computers, telecommunication, and the internet are putting power in the hands of the customer and giving relief to CSRs. What are some of these advances?

1.) The Phone Menu

2.) Automated Phone Interfacing

3.) Web Based

4.) Artificial Intelligence

The Phone Menu

The phone menu is the first notable change in the process of customers contacting a company. You have all heard people say "I hate menus" or "I just press 0 to get through to someone." However, Phone Menus do allow a vast majority of callers to go directly to the specific departments they need. This allows the company to turn the negative perception around and "selective" customer service can take place. A firm can also allocate their human resources more efficiently.

Note to management – Keep the path of phone menus as simple as possible. Menus that are too intricate and require too many "punches" can frustrate the customer.

Automated Phone Interfacing

Automated phone interfacing is the next step over phone menus. Banks and investment firms are excellent examples of business models implementing this tool. In these cases, the customer actually punches in account information and receives return information such as account balance, recent checks cleared, etc. Depending on the information the customer is looking for, it may not be necessary for them to talk to a live agent. If the procedure is fast and simple, and the customer can receive the information they need, feedback on this tool can be very positive.

Web Based

Web Based is another higher advancement. As so many people are behind a computer throughout the day with internet access, web based customer interfacing is becoming very popular and by many, preferred. Customers can contact a company while sitting at their desk. The usual procedure is for the customer to sign up with his own pass code on the company's web site. After this is done, the customer can perform a host of tasks they could only do before while speaking to a CSR. Also, the customer may have the opportunity to speak to a CSR through email or in a chat room. This can result in a great cost savings for the company as the CSR may be able to interface with more than one customer at the same time through this method. Software and computer companies' web sites usually have online chats where the customer can receive real time technical advice through a virtual conversation. Speed and simplicity make these websites very popular, along with putting the customer in the driver's seat.

Artificial Intelligence

Finally, Artificial Intelligence is still a growing baby. Already most of us have experienced talking to computers over the phone when calling information or airlines. As the technology in this arena improves, we will literally be holding full conversations with computers to work out tasks and issues. I engaged one the other day talking to a bank over the phone and the conversation was close to having one with a live person.

Again, it is up to the firm to do their own cost and marketing analysis to determine which of the aforementioned they wish to invest in. One thing to keep in mind, the Customer Service Representative will never be totally replaced. Will the computer be able to "think outside the box" like a CSR can? Will the computer keep a "smiling tone" in the voice when the customer calls in very upset? Will the computer be able to take control of the call after the customer has vented for five minutes, and come up with the proper solution? The Human Resource is still the most valuable commodity any corporation holds.

Chapter 7

Think Internal, not only External!

Customer Service Representatives are in a unique position as they deal with customers on a daily basis. They speak to them on their best and worst days, hearing the callers' likes, dislikes, and needs. The knowledge and understanding CSRs obtain on their customer base is higher than most realize.

This knowledge should always be utilized and channeled to the CSR's most important "internal" customer, the manager. Yes, your manager is your boss, but at the same time is an internal customer who needs your feedback. They need to hear what the customers are saying, and channel this information to the decision-makers of the company (upper management).

Note to management – Always keep the door open to listening to your employees concerning customer concerns, issues, and patterns. Keep your door open to upper management as well to channel this information upward.

Customer trends and attitudes about certain services or products become apparent when Customer Representatives pass them on to management. Management can keep a log of these trends and form a think tank to address them.

"Internal" relationships can also exist with other CSRs in the way of Mentor and Protégé. The CSR may speak with other departments daily such as Customer Relations and Billing. Customer Reps should treat all of these relationships with the same K's and P's discussed earlier for External Customers.

Excellent communication between Customer Service and other departments is essential. Aside from Sales, Customer Service has the pulse of the customer. Customer Service Representatives may be sensing a trend among customers concerning opinions toward your firm or products without even realizing it. Management should provide a proper setting and atmosphere to ask CSRs pertinent questions which may uncover these customer concerns.

"Have you noticed any consistent feedback regarding our products?"

"Do customers like our new format?"

Regular meetings with customer service representatives and their managers will accomplish this. Other Departments heads may wish to attend these meetings to gain information and insight.

Chapter 8

Employee versus Contractor? The Results should be the same!

Some corporations today contract out their customer service departments to third party companies. When a consumer calls customer service they are actually speaking to another company representing the one they think they're calling.

Given the importance of customer service, it is preferable to have a more direct relationship whenever possible and the customer service agent work directly for the company they're representing. However, the contractor relationship can be very effective as long as certain factors are in place between the two companies.

1.) Full Training

2.) Expectations and Protocol

3.) Open communication

Full Training

It is imperative the C.S.A. receive full training on the products and services he or she will be asked about. The C.S.A. should know the products as if he/she was a full time employee for years with the company represented. Training throughout the year on new products and changes to current services should also take place. The contractor C.S.A. does not want to hear about a new product from the customer before he or she knows about it.

Expectations and Protocol

The Corporation should fully disclose their expectations for the hired customer service vendor in the areas of customer interfacing. These include duties such as greeting, script, and boundaries of agent empowerment. The contracted C.S.A. should know exactly what the duties entail and the limits thereof.

Open Communication

For all of this to happen, there must be open communication between the vendor and hiring corporation. Weekly conference calls between management, regular face-to-face meetings, and daily calls between the two are a good idea. Both companies have a dependent relationship with each other and need to nurture this relationship to guarantee positive results.

The contractor CSR is in a unique position where two internal customers are being served (the company they work for and the company they represent over the phone). Remember, there is still only ONE External Customer in all of this. The Contractor CSR must focus on the External Customer even more. In the Customer's eyes good customer service is always appreciated but also expected, and insufficient service is quickly noticed. The same goal should still be sought after every call – Total Customer Fulfillment!

Chapter 9

Face-to-Face Service

Face-to-face and over-the-counter customer service in the retail market bring in other factors the store owner, retail clerk on the floor, cashier, and customer service counter should keep in mind. The "K's and P's" should still be utilized, however now there is also direct contact taking place with the customer. Other important factors to remember are:

1.) Eye Contact

2.) Body Language

3.) Physical Appearance

4.) Availability

5.) Policy Knowledge

Eye Contact

Make frequent eye contact with the customer without staring or glaring. Assure them through this eye contact you are listening to their words, care about their questions, and are paying attention to their wants. Come up with the proper solution they need.

Body Language

Avoid quick and sudden movements, or the appearance of being rushed. Customers can pick up subliminal signals in face-to-face transactions and can tell the kind of day you're having. If you're having a bad day, make an extra effort to put "calmness" into your demeanor through how you walk, speak, and your movements. You never want the customer to take the kind of day you're having personally.

Physical Appearance

"Be professional in appearance" we've all heard before. If you do not wear a uniform on the floor, always dress according to the guidelines set forth by your business. You're representing this business to everyone who walks through the door, and "a picture is truly worth a thousand words."

Availability

Be available to customers whenever possible. If you notice that customer flow is too high on the floor, over the cashier desk, or at the customer service counter, please communicate with management. I've never met a customer yet who likes to wait in lines.

Note to Retail Management — Please keep communication open between you and your retail personnel. Listen to their feedback regarding customer flow and "hot times" when extra help or back-up may be needed.

Overall the concepts of Face-to-Face Customer Service coincide with Customer Service over the phone but do have added features. Retail Sales, the Hotel Industry, and other businesses require the employee to hone all of the above people skills. Meet the challenge, and represent your company well!

Chapter 10

Selling in the Service Call

The Customer Service Representative does sell the company and all of its products/services on every call. The CSR's demeanor and professionalism may determine if they will generate repeat or new business. Outside of this "indirect selling," the C.S.R. may also venture into "direct sales" and actually promote new products, services, or specials.

It should be remembered when customers call customer service they are calling for specific reasons, and usually do not intend to hear a sales script. However, the customer service call can be a great opportunity for promotion of a product when done correctly.

The sales pitch in customer service should be done with the following in mind:

1.) Finding the Moment

2.) Efficient

3.) Periodic

Finding the Moment

The Customer Rep should always remember to address the reasons the consumer called customer service first. Once all of these needs are met, the sales pitch can then begin. Usually the opportune moment for this is toward the end of the call. At times it can be done in the middle of the call if the Customer Rep is waiting for a customer process to be done on the computer terminal.

Efficient

Keep the sales pitch short and sweet.

"Would you like to hear about our special offer today, sir?"

Or

"We have a new product coming out next week your company may be interested in. Would you like to hear about it?"

Both of these examples are low pressure sales toward the customer and give them the power to pursue the offer or not. There may be a different pitch for different customers based on which products your company is promoting and which customers call in. In other words, "the right fit" should be kept in mind.

Periodic

It may be a good idea to have customer service direct sell only at certain times of the year, or for only given lengths of time. Customers may not want a sales pitch every time they call.

Note to Management — Added incentives are a good way to increase corporate revenue, and also motivate the work force. A little reimbursement for every Customer Rep who makes a sale or reaches a sales goal can bring a new dimension to the job.

When you are in customer service, performing sales on the call may at first feel like an added burden or just something extra to do. However, by incorporating the sales pitch into your "muscle memory," it will become more natural and rewarding. Actually seeing company revenue increase because of your efforts is a thrill. Besides, there may be a sales professional in you without your knowing it!

Many cashier clerks in retail are using the sales pitch during check out in an effort to gain one more sale. I was in a drug store the other day purchasing some paper towels and the cashier asked if I would like to try their new chocolate chip cookies which were stacked right there at the counter. They looked so good I impulsively bought two packs even though I had no intention of buying any food, and it was all because of a very short sales proposal.

Chapter 11

Oh Sales...Don't Forget the Service!

Now more than ever before, Professional Sales need to remember the importance of customer service. Large retail hardware, clothing, and other chains have incorporated customer service into all of their retail sales procedures for years. Retail Sales Reps know their products and the needs of their customers, and are prepared to answer their questions during the sales process and afterward. The smaller stores selling the same thing stay in business <u>because</u> of their customer service.

Professional Sales can also quickly find the value in Customer Service!

Field Sales and Inside Sales need to keep in mind F.E.M.

1.) Follow-up

2.) Educate

3.) Maintain

Follow-up

Certain sales teams deal directly with end users and sell a product almost classified as "one time only." My brother recently bought an appliance for his home through a field sales representative. Although the appliance has a great guarantee and will probably last twenty years, the sales rep should make a follow-up call with my brother in the next month to see how the installation went and if my brother is satisfied with the product. Why? My brother will be impressed with his follow-up and service. He will also be more likely to tell others about this and hence give the sales professional "word of mouth advertising." Also, my brother could always end up moving and need another appliance – who would he think of calling first? Could the new and used car salesman find the value in customer follow-up?

Educate

Sales Professionals have many expectations in today's world. To gain new business, keep the current business, perform and keep track of administrative duties, and directives from management, entertainments, and more. Time management is essential!

The closing process of any sales professional should include educating the customer on customer service numbers to call when needed. In other words, the Account Executive, (AE) wants to convey to the customer all processes in place relating to the product or service they are purchasing. The customer should be informed that if any roadblocks occur that the processes in place do not address sufficiently, he or she should feel free to call the AE. Why? If the frustration level of customers rises too high, they may end up looking at the competition as an alternative. It is also much easier to retain a current customer than to go out and find one to replace them. More energy and time is used in the latter.

The "Follow-up" calls for new ongoing customers should be frequent in the beginning, then once every week or every other week, and finally spread out in time. Providing education on the product, service, or processes can also be accomplished during these calls. "Spoon Feeding" on each call may work very well depending on how complicated or vast the scope is of the products/services the customers have purchased.

Maintain

Maintaining your current customer base begins with a combination of the "Follow-up" and "Educate." These are the starting factors of the "personal relationship" every sales pro wants to have with their clients. If a customer is happy, calls start to have more to do with new products and services (future sales) than with the current product they have. Also, the AE will find himself talking more about the customer's new baby or asking questions like "So how was your getaway this weekend?" Entertainment solidifies the relationship even more. A good personal professional relationship is good business!

Note to Sales Management – Relay the importance of FEM to your sales force.

FEM may produce two things in the end: a satisfied customer base and more sales! A little more customer service incorporated into your sales process can make you stand out from the competition in your customers' eyes. It will also keep you in touch with their needs. Relaying these needs to upper management through your manager is a great idea as Upper Management make decisions on new products and processes. Hearing customer feedback can help put their decision-making on target!

Note to Sales Management – The notion that if a person does a good job in customer service, he or she may not do well in sales because they'll be doing more servicing than selling, is being reassessed. Many good customer service agents have later proved themselves in the sales force (myself included). Many CSRs may have a strong desire to sell as their next career challenge. Training to get them more in the selling mode along with their already present service mindset may allow them to perform at their best. Keep this in mind during your next set of interviews for an open territory.

Chapter 12

"Notes to Management"

Many notes to management have been discussed in this book. Let us review them:

Note to management – Make sure everyone at the company realizes the importance of what they do, and how it eventually affects the customer.

Note to management – Training Customer Reps on your companies' products should be fully covered in C.S. training. Also, regular training throughout the year on current and new products is highly recommended.

Note to management – Recognize the Customer Representatives who have done their job for some time and done it well. Awards and promotions within customer service give the agent something to strive for, and increases morale. It can also reduce Manager Transfer calls.

Note to management – Recognize the need for MPUB, (Mentally Prepare, Pace Yourself, Utilize Breaks, and have a Back-Up Plan), and help your CSRs in any area they need. You may have different suggestions for each individual to help them deal with the day-to-day stress of customer service.

Note to management – Make sure Customer Service Representatives understand they are truly "representing" their entire company, just as sales professionals do in the field. Their actions can affect the bottom line as much as revenue generating departments.

Note to management – Keep the path of phone menus as simple as possible. Menus which are too intricate and require too many "punches" can create frustration on the part of the customer.

Note to management – Always keep the door open to listening to your employees concerning customer concerns, issues, and patterns. Keep your door open to upper management as well to channel this information up.

Note to Retail Management – Please keep communication open between you and your retail personnel. Listen to their feedback regarding customer flow and "hot times" when extra help or back-up may be needed.

Note to Management – Added incentives are a good way to increase corporate revenue, and also motivate the work force. A little reimbursement for every Customer Rep who makes a sale or reaches a sales goal can bring a new, positive dimension to the job.

Note to Sales Management – Relay the importance of FEM to your sales force, (Book I, Chapter 11).

Note to Sales Management – The notion that if a person does a good job in customer service, he or she may not do well in sales because they'll be doing more servicing than selling, is being reassessed. Many good customer service agents have later proved themselves in the sales force (myself included). Many CSRs may have a strong desire to sell as their next career challenge. Training to get them more in the selling mode along with their already present FEM Mindset can help them excel. Keep this in mind during your next set of interviews for an open territory.

All of the above add up to four things: Management taking care of their most important internal customers (their employees), management making their corporation a stronger company, management allowing better service for external customers, and increased sales. Managers who accomplish the aforementioned are certainly performing well in the most important aspects of their job. They are removing barriers hindering employee performance and improving company processes already in place. Managers who can take these steps and keep a positive frame of mind during stressful times are usually popular, and employees want to work for them. Also, the work productivity of these groups can be high. People-oriented management pays off!

Chapter 13

An Attitude of Service

What exactly is "An Attitude of Service?" The Service Attitude is the mindset every employee should have. It is a realization that their actions do affect their Ultimate Customers either directly or indirectly. It is an awareness their work will add value to the products presented to their customers. It is a desire to do the best job possible on their end in an effort to bring the best possible service to their Customers.

A good Customer Service Representative has a strong Service Attitude. Practicing the 4 K's and P's of Service, utilizing Agent Empowerment, "feeding" Internal Customers are all ways of maintaining an Attitude of Service. Face-to-Face Customer Service entails all of the aforementioned along with a good sense of your use of body language, physical appearance, and professional demeanor.

Customer Service can be the most rewarding when CSRs actually see their efforts help customers and the customers hang up the phone appreciative of that help. What better feeling is there in solving a customer's problems than turning a troubled consumer into a totally satisfied one? The challenge of Customer Service is to maintain a good Service Attitude in the midst of repetitive daily calls, and problem calls. By utilizing all of the concepts discussed earlier, discouragement can be overcome!

Upper Management is faced with pressures and challenges from many sides. Stock Holders' expectations (for profit), taking care of employees, customer expectations, new product ideas/enactment, and making their company a quality firm are all on the table. "An Attitude of Service" can aid the Senior Vice-President in developing a way to simplify all of these goals and challenges. Upper Management can spend time with CSRs directly interfacing with the customer or ride with Sales Professionals out in the field. This is the chance to hear feedback directly from Ultimate Customers regarding your firm's products, services, and procedures. The CSR and Sales Professional can also give you direct feedback on issues and tell you what other customers think about these areas as well. This is the knowledge you need before round-tabling new ideas or changes to current methods in place. The strategies that can come from "tag alongs" can inject more potency into your company and address many or all of the challenges you face. So, please stay in contact with Mr. Customer Service Representative or Ms. Sales Professional.

Mid-Level/Front Line Management needs to keep the channels of communication open above and below you. You may directly interface with the Ultimate Customer from time to time, but the CSRs will be doing much more. You are the channel for the customer trends/desires they notice to go to Upper Management. Have a good relationship with your employees so they may always approach you with these trends, and keep the door open to those above you. Take care of your employees (internal customers) while listening to their needs and removing barriers to that communication.

Sales Professionals should never forget the importance of Customer Service. What better way to impress your customer base than by letting them know you will be there for them after they sign? Good service will help bring about a good professional personal relationship, which is what you want.

Finding your "Attitude of Service" is a goal every employee should want to have regardless of the position he or she holds. Maintaining your "Attitude of Service" is just as important. Find and maintain your Service Attitude and see if your work does not seem to have a little more value, the job has a little more importance, and your direction is a little more focused. Someone once said "In losing yourself you find yourself" What better way to "lose yourself" than in servicing and helping others? Some of the greatest people in history took this approach. Can you think of anyone?

Book II

<u>The Handbook of Sales for More Business</u>

Roger Reynold

Table of Contents

Book II – The Handbook of Sales for More Business

Dedication 61

Introduction 63

Chapter 1) Attributes of Successful Sales Professionals 65

Chapter 2) Relationship Building 71

Chapter 3) Don't Forget the Service! 75

Chapter 4) Persistence, Rejection, Performance 79

Chapter 5) Bring Your Own Personality 83

Chapter 6) Retaining instead of Neglecting 87

Chapter 7) Grow the Business 91

Chapter 8) Keep it Simple 95

Chapter 9) Seniors, help the Juniors 99

Dedication

This book is dedicated to all Sales People who represent their firms with professionalism and integrity on a daily basis. It is also for those Sales Professionals who want to make a positive impact with their customers through trusting relationships.

Introduction to Book Two

The Handbook of Sales for More Business outlines many ingredients found in stronger customer relationships and higher sales. The Sales Clerk behind the Counter, Inside Sales Executive over the phone, or Sales Professional out in the field should find this beneficial.

Although the length of the Sales Relationship may differ in all of the above positions, this Handbook can outline a sales foundation for all of them. The chapters can give insight into the successful sales professional and improve performance in various types of sales.

Chapter 1

Attributes of Successful
Sales Professionals

Whether you're behind a retail counter, an inside sales representative working over the phone, or field sales professional with a Fortune 500 Firm, many common attributes are shared among successful sales people. Let us first list and discuss these traits to lay a strong foundation for a successful career in sales.

The common personality traits of Successful Sales Professionals are:

    1.) People person

    2.) Positive personality

    3.) Purpose driven

    4.) Thrilled by the close

The People Person

Did you ever notice how some people have a knack for making others feel comfortable? Do you have an aunt or uncle in your family who seems to get along with everyone and has a lot of friends? People like this are usually People Persons, individuals who genuinely enjoy being around others, meeting new people, and have the ability to build a relationship with them if the situation and time allow.

People Persons are natural sales representatives. They enjoy interaction with their fellow man, and have a way of letting the other know he/she cares about what they're going through. They let an individual or group express themselves as needed, and are good listeners.

Do you have a desire to be in sales, have many friends, and have developed a number of positive relationships? If so there is a People Person within you. Sometimes personality traits such as shyness, impatience, or self-centeredness can get in the way of bringing the "People Person" in you to the surface. Take an honest look at yourself and strive to find ways to overcome your own barriers to being more of a People Person.

Take a greater interest in your current relationships by listening to others more often. People love to talk about themselves, and in today's stressful world people need someone to talk to. Defeat your shyness by meeting new people through your contacts with current friends or family. After this, try to start a conversation with a total stranger while waiting in line or coming out of church. Work on making the People Person within you stronger; you'll be glad you did.

Positive Personality

It is way too easy in today's age to think or act negatively. "It may rain today," "I don't like him," "When is this day going to end?"

Good sales professionals are positive people. They look for the positive in others, and always try to build up rather than tear down. Positive people recognize human fallibility, and have a good self image. They try not to judge, and follow the Golden Rule. Even negative people enjoy being around positive people because they usually experience something in the relationship that may have been missing when they grew up, or is missing in current friend/family relationships.

Good sales people use more positive language, always see the glass as half-full, and inherently pass this positive mental attitude on to others. Try to recognize when you speak or act negatively with others, and use more positive phrases. Changing your habits brings a changed outcome in every interaction.

Good sales people can enter negative situations and remain positive/professional through the employment of a good tone of voice, a calm demeanor, and by expressing a genuine concern about the other's experience. The store clerk dealing with the return, inside sales representative talking to an angry customer, or field sales professional face-to-face with an upset customer should all maintain a positive and professional attitude.

"I'm sorry you went through that, Mr. Customer. Please tell me exactly what happened, what the issues are, and I will address them."

Or

"I don't blame you for being upset. You and your business mean a lot to us and I do apologize for this inconvenience."

The successful salesman concentrates on two things in these situations: How important the relationship is, and meeting the issues affecting the relationship head on. This can involve rolling up your sleeves and utilizing some of the fundamentals of customer service, but doing all you can to resolve the customer's dilemma should improve your relationship with the customer, even if the situation cannot be totally reversed. You will find a chapter later in this book about customer service in sales.

Purpose Driven

I started in Customer Service, performed my duties well, and later became a field sales professional winning numerous sales accolades. When I became a Sales Professional, I reprogrammed my thinking processes to focus on two main goals or purposes:

    a. Keep the current business on board

    b. Gain new business

The outlook that if you're good in customer service you may have the wrong mindset to excel in sales has been proven wrong. When moving from customer service to sales, I considered my customer service skills as an advantage to keep current business on board. It takes much more energy to get an account back once it is lost, or to open an account to make up for one lost. Keep your customer base happy and satisfied, and you'll have a good start in surpassing your sales goals.

Taking care of my base became a routine of mine, and is explored in greater detail in the following chapter.

Every week when I went into the field, I made it a short term goal to either close on new business, close on incremental business from current customers, or to make headway in the sales process with a prospective new customer. Some closes may take much longer than others depending on the size and scope of the account or industry.

Further ingredients of the Purpose Driven mindset are a good knowledge of the product or service you are selling, and belief in this product/service to make a positive difference with your customer in his/her business. The prospective new customer may eventually disagree with your sales presentation if you do not believe in what you're selling, and do not know the product you're selling inside and out. Your presentation will reveal if there is enthusiasm and excitement behind your words. Prospects' questions will reveal if they have deeper product knowledge after your presentation is completed. The successful sales professional must come through on each one!

Thrilled by the close

Most all successful sales professionals really enjoy what they do. I always admired the professional baseball or football player. Almost all of them are doing what they really love, and tap into experiences going back to childhood. Hitting that home run or throwing the touchdown pass gives instant positive feedback. A "thrill" or "healthy rush" is experienced, along with a sense of accomplishment. The ballplayer not only helped the team out, but brought some enthusiasm to the crowd, a success for them to root for. The accomplished musician experiences the same phenomenon when performing. The musician gives the audience a pleasurable experience and temporary escape from their daily responsibilities. At the same time, he/she is part of a team and participating in the team's success.

A successful career in sales parallels the above very closely. Any sales person is part of a bigger team (the company they work for). They are trying to make the team stronger through closing new business, and bring something positive to their audience (bringing their product or service to new and existing customers). Competition is there in the form of other corporations selling similar products or services. You know, however, their product is inferior because they don't have you selling for them! Who else can gain new business and take care of your customers like you will?

Did you have a positive feeling when you made a good trade as a child, or sold your first cup of lemonade at the end of your driveway? That is the Thrill of the Close we've been discussing. It's the winning home run or touchdown pass. The sales person just made her company stronger, made a positive change for her customer, and increased her own monetary position. A win/win/win scenario if there ever was one! You'll know right away when you experience the Thrill of the Close.

Chapter 2

Relationship Building

Relationship Building is the essence of all sales. It may be very short term as in the retail sales experience, or longer term as in field sales. The commonality is: good sales relationships foster trust and more business.

Short Term Sales Relationships

Retail Salespeople are in a unique position as they may only have one chance to close business. The First Impression is huge. Their face-to-face encounter brings importance to the greeting, tone of voice, body language, and demeanor. All of these bullet points are important in every form of sales, although the Inside Sales Representative will not have to be concerned with body language.

Good retail or inside sales people may have made such a good impression, that the customer may come back again and seek out the same individual. This is the ultimate positive feedback a sales person can receive. The first customer interaction was so positive that the customer is giving repeat business to the same company. He may not even realize it may have more to do with the sales person than with the product itself, but they both are part of what the company is offering.

Long Term Sales Relationships

These relationships may be more common in Corporate Inside Sales and Field Sales. The Sales Executive will probably have a set territory, customer base and prospect list. The Sales professional is responsible for maintaining and growing the current customer base, as well as bringing new customers on board within the territory.

Building on current relationships and developing new relationships are the keys to dealing with the customer base and prospects.

Current customer relationships still need to be fed to keep them alive and fresh. Never take your customer's business for granted, as there are always other alternatives. Here are some insightful ways to both grow and keep a strong customer relationship.

1.) Regular sales calls with your current customers

2.) Their pain is your pain attitude

3.) Remind them of the value they are receiving

Regular sales calls can allow you to stand out from the competition. How many sales professionals fade into the sunset after the close is made? How many sales people are hard to get hold of once this is done? Regular sales calls allow you to stay in touch with what your customer is thinking and feeling, and may open the door to incremental sales down the road. The regular visits may go from always talking about their business, to asking about their family. Good sales professionals can't help but build a personal professional relationship with their contacts, and they may even become friends.

Regular sales calls allow you to penetrate the company further, and gain more contacts. A number of contacts I've had with companies have changed over the years, and in many cases pro-active penetration allowed me to already have a relationship with the new contact. Don't take for granted that the current decision-maker will always be there.

The regular sales call can allow you to discover any growing issues the customer is experiencing before they become deal-breaking. Are they having trouble getting through to our customer service department? Did one of our products not meet their standards? Catching problems early allows better resolutions, just as in the health care field. Let them know you actually care about what they are experiencing. If they are upset, you share in their pain. Many of my customers started to think of me as working for them, even joking they would be getting a desk for me to use whenever I stopped in. This just shows the relationship is strong, I've paid attention to the account, and the trust can then follow.

Make sure the customer knows what you're doing for them in the current customer relationship. From time to time, you may want to make a presentation outlining the calls you've made, company performance, and issues you've addressed. This presentation may include a mention of the new products your firm is offering that the customer may be interested in. Demonstrate to your customer that you have a partnership, and a <u>mutually beneficial relationship!</u>

Building new relationships may involve cold calling, but certainly a first time meeting. The first impression can only happen once, so always look professional and impressive. Be confident in what you're selling. Remember, you already know your product will help the company or individual you're calling on, and you have excellent product knowledge. With a firm handshake, present your business card, maintain eye contact, and then gain their confidence by stating your purpose. Allow them to talk about their needs and their company needs. Repeat some of their words to reinforce you've been listening and care about what they're saying. When the opportunity is right, ask them if you may come back and present a formal proposal. If your product has a short sales cycle, go for the close right there. Longer cycles may require another meeting and possibly another one after that.

Remember, no sales call is ever wasted. The more a prospect interfaces with you, the more you are building a relationship and possibly gaining a future customer. People do look for a connection with others, and the more your prospects connect with you, the greater the chance of closes.

Chapter 3

Don't Forget the Service!

Now more than ever before, Professional Sales need to keep in mind the importance of customer service. Large retail hardware, clothing, and other chains have incorporated customer service into all of their retail sales procedures for years. Retail Sales Reps know their products and the needs of their customers, and are prepared to answer their questions during the sales process and afterward. The smaller stores selling the same thing stay in business <u>because</u> of their customer service.

Professional Sales can also quickly find the value in Customer Service!

Field Sales and Inside Sales need to keep in mind F.E.M.

1.) Follow-up

2.) Educate

3.) Maintain

Follow-up

There are field sales forces that deal directly with end users and sell a product almost classified as "one time only." Again, my brother recently bought an appliance for his home through a field sales representative. Although the appliance has a great guarantee and will probably last twenty years, the sales rep should make a follow-up call with my brother in the next month to see how the installation went and if my brother is satisfied with the product. Why? My brother will be impressed with his follow-up and service. He will also be more likely to tell others about this and hence give the sales professional "word of mouth advertising." Also, my brother could always end up moving and need another appliance – who would he think of calling first? The new and used car salesmen are finding value in the customer follow-up that can generate new and repeat business.

The Follow-up with customers who purchase an ongoing service or consumable product is even more important. Don't assume their business will always stay in your bucket. The only way to ensure this is the follow-up call after the close and regular sales calls afterward.

Educate

Sales Professionals have many expectations in today's world: to gain new business, keep the current business, perform administrative duties, and follow directives from management, offer entertainment, and more. Time management is essential!

The closing process of any sales professional should include educating the customer on customer service numbers to call when needed. In other words, the Account Executive wants to convey to the customer all processes in place relating to the product or service they are purchasing. The AE is a limited resource and the customer will receive a faster response going through the proper channels. However, the customer should be informed that if any large road blocks occur where the processes in place do not suffice in addressing those blocks, he or she is to call the AE. Why? If the frustration level of customers goes too high, they may end up looking at the competition as an alternative. Remember, it is much easier to retain a current customer than to go out and find one to replace them. More energy and time is used in the latter.

The "Follow-up" calls for new ongoing customers should be frequent in the beginning, once every week or every other week, then spread out as time goes on. Educating the customer on the product, service, or processes can also be done during these calls. "Spoon Feeding" on each call may work very well depending on how complicated or vast the scope is of the products/services he or she purchased.

Maintain

Maintaining your current customer base begins with a combination of "Follow-up" and "Educate." These are the starting factors of the "personal relationship" every sales professional wants to have with their clients and was discussed in the previous chapter. Entertainment solidifies the relationship. A good personal relationship is good business!

Note to Sales Management – Relay the importance of FEM to your sales force.

FEM can produce two things in the end: a satisfied customer base and more sales! A little more customer service balanced with customer education incorporated into your sales process can make you stand out in the customer's eyes from other competitors. It can also keep you in touch with their needs. Relaying these needs to upper management through your manager is a great idea as upper management makes decisions on new products and processes. Hearing customer feedback and information on their needs can keep management's decision-making on target!

Chapter 4

Persistence, Rejection, Performance

There is an additional trait to the successful Sales Professional's Personality that deserves its own chapter, Persistence! This trait is not unique to sales however. Most all individuals at the top of their game have this quality. It may be demonstrated in the work ethic of the professional athlete in frequency and intensity of practice. It is common that athletes with the best statistics in their sports partake in above average practice and coaching sessions. Well known authors, movie producers, and artists are totally dedicated to their field. Time and sweat go into each piece of work until it is just right. These are all forms of Persistence which can bring outstanding results.

Inevitably, the persistent sales personality will have to deal with a certain kind of feedback, even more so than the above careers. This feedback is rejection. Rejection can go hand-in-hand with Persistence in sales. How many closes have occurred because the Account Executive would not give up, and kept calling on the same prospect? All the time we hear stories about closes taking one, two, or even three years or more.

Persistence drives the Sales Professional to gain a higher level in the prospect relationship. When the prospect is not willing to go through the sales cycle at all, the sales professional may put them on the "C" List and lower the call frequency.

However, he still watches for any positive change in the relationship. Maybe three months from now the decision-maker will come out to talk to me? Maybe the decision-maker will be willing to make a future appointment? Persistence can allow this to happen, and may catch the prospect at a time when their current provider has failed. In this case, <u>timing plus persistence trumps rejection</u>!

Persistence does give way to Performance and higher sales, but how do you handle rejection along the way? You are human, you have feelings and are not a robot, so what do you do with rejection?

First, recognize no one likes rejection, which goes back to everyone's childhood. How many times did you attempt something and wanted to succeed to gain your family's pat on the back? Were you worried how they would react if you failed? How nervous were you when you asked your first date out or even went on your first date, afraid they may not like you? Answer: take stock in yourself! Remember the Successful Sales Professional is:

a. Offering a product or service that will help your prospect

b. Offering a solid product knowledge

You're doing them a favor by calling on them! Don't take rejection personally, but recognize people can be creatures of habit and want to stay with their current provider, even though yours is better. People can also be rushed, feel over worked, be going through a difficult situation in their personal life, the list is endless. Many times the rejection is a reflection of this, and has nothing to do with you or your sales approach.

The key phrase my mind always brings to the forefront with any rejection or negative feedback is "Stay Professional." This phrase got me through many a time in Customer Service, Sales, and Management. When a current customer is angry about something and may even be venting at you, Stay Professional. Recognize what is happening, acknowledge their feelings, and see what you can do to rectify the situation. When the prospect may even be rude saying he does not have time for you, Stay Professional. Thank him in advance for any future opportunity to meet, and leave your contact information.

Closes from any accounts like these are really accomplishments you can take pride in. Your own persistence, handling the rejection, your sales skills allowed you to eventually make the close. Some closes are easier than others, sometimes called low hanging fruit. These are always welcome and help make your sales goals. However, closes that come from accounts who did not even want to see you in the beginning are quite an achievement. That is why you are special in what you do!

Chapter 5

Bring Your Own Personality

Almost every Fortune 500 Firm will provide sales training. It may be a step-by-step approach regarding what to do in the sales cycle. Smaller companies may do this, and the practice is also applicable to Inside Sales. Training is an excellent method of improving your sales skills in areas such as probing, overcoming objections, and so on. The format your superiors want you to use is the format which should be implemented, but don't forget to "Bring Your Own Personality" to the table!

A common occurrence with new sales executives is they stick to the script or sales steps to a tee. This is perfectly understandable as they are trying to find their way and want to do a good job. As time goes on, they settle down, and the sales presentation is not as rigid and becomes more personable. The new Account Executive realizes the person at the other end may not want to follow the formatted sales steps. The new AE learns to balance what the customer wants while taking control of the sales call. Remember: good Account Executives are good listeners!

The main goal is to develop a positive professional relationship with the customer that results in a close. Customers and prospects today are looking for real people that say what they mean and mean what they say. Belief in your product and product knowledge will help you bring genuineness to the sales process, and believe me the customers should respect that.

Aside from that, bring your own personality based on your life experiences. Search your own interests to help find commonality with the prospect. I am an avid golfer, which is very common in the business world. Many of my customers either play golf regularly, or watch the bigger tournaments on television. Many, however, don't, and want to talk about something else. I also have an interest in baseball and football, but that may not interest them either. Look around their office for clues. One call I made had three pictures of horses on the desk. The prospect's daughter was really into horse jumping. I spent five summers at my grandpa's horse farm where I learned to ride and even rope a little. After mentioning this we were "off to the races." The call was broken down into fifteen minutes of fact finding, and twenty-five minutes of talking about horses. I easily got permission to come back and present a proposal the following week. With that, the business was on board.

Keep in mind that now more than ever before, customers are pressed for time. You'll know in your conversation if the customer just wants to stick to business, or has time to talk about something else as well. It still won't hurt to mention the pictures of horses on his desk, but he may not have time to talk at length about them. It all comes down again to "listening" to the customer and finding the right balance.

Aside from talking about common interests and experiences, what other ways can you use your own personality to your advantage? Be creative. My friend Jerry in pharmaceutical sales called on a customer some months back who told

Jerry he was experiencing lower back pain. He could definitely identify with this as he had the same problem. When Jerry got home, he pulled a few sheets from his file on back pain, and also bought a sports muscle rub for his customer that had worked before. He brought them in the next morning and put them on his desk before he came in. It took two hours before the customer sent him an email. He was so appreciative, telling my friend he had already applied the salve and could feel relief. The stretching exercises he was going to try when he got home. I believe that was the first time my friend ever did anything like that for a customer. What just took place here?

    a. A creative out-of-the-box gesture was offered

    b. The customer found value in this gesture

    c. The sales professional customer relationship was cemented

How many other vendors will not only take an interest in what the customer is personally experiencing, but is also willing to do something about it? Little acts of kindness like this are a plus for a customer. The benefit is it may keep the business on board for a long time.

Another friend of mine also in sales had a customer who was really into NASCAR. His contact was new to the company and told him about his interest after NASCAR season was over. He also told my friend who his favorite driver was. A light bulb went off and my friend remembered seeing die cast NASCAR model cars at his local pharmacy. He went to the pharmacy and found the exact car of his favorite driver in 1/24 scale for only ten dollars. He presented it to him in a meeting the following week, and his customer could not say enough about it. All of a sudden it was like they had known each other for years! A little gesture like this can go a long way in the business relationship. Another sales professional I knew was an excellent cook and she made her customers brownies. Now there is another good example of bringing a personal touch to the business relationship!

Finally, avoid any topics of discussion which may come back to haunt you. You may both have an interest in politics, but if you did not vote for the same candidates...enough said. Temper all of your discussions with common sense, and always remember the key phrase..."Stay Professional."

Chapter 6

Retaining instead of Neglecting

As we discussed earlier, retaining and taking care of your base accounts should be number one on your list. The amount of time and money needed to bring an account back once it is lost or having to open another one to make up for it is huge. Let us recap all of the ways to retain your base:

1.) Regular customer calls

2.) You have an excellent product knowledge and are prepared to help the customer on every call

3.) You are not afraid to get involved with a customer service issue if the regular customer service process did not satisfy them

4.) You keep the customer abreast of new products and services which will benefit them

5.) Meeting with the customer from time to time re-capping the job performance you and your firm have done for them, and any other useful data for the customer

6.) Creative gestures

7.) Entertainment

8.) Developing a strong professional relationship from all of the above

Entertainment was touched on in the previous chapter talking about some of the out-of-the-box creative gestures you can do for your customer. Putting their interests first and getting them something that adds to those interests can go a long way. This may even hit home more than a new coffee mug with your company logo on it. These giveaways however should not be forgotten because having anything in their office with your company name on it is good business. It reminds them of the mutually beneficial relationship that exists between the two firms, and the positive relationship between you and your contact.

More formal entertainment such as lunches, dinners, golf outings, and customer outings should always be considered if the budget allows. Many times the customer does not have time to go to lunch or may be not allowed to go out with vendors. Bringing food to them is usually accepted, and does hit home. Customers really look forward to even simple drop-offs like donuts or bagels. My friend Rick who sold electronics called me one day and said he had a customer whose president he met with once a quarter but was having trouble making a true connection. I asked him if he knew what kind of food he liked. Rick could only remember him eating a bagel once. So, after a common sense suggestion, my friend brought in a box of bagels with three different cream cheeses for the President and his staff. The connection was made, and the President even called him on the phone three weeks later asking when he was going to bring in more as it "had been a while". The next day he was there, bagels in hand, and made sure his business card was on each box.

Another positive outcome of bringing food to a company is that it allows more than a select few to participate as opposed to a lunch or dinner. Everyone asks who brought the donuts, bagels, or pizza? They end up hearing your name as well as your company name, and have a "good taste in their mouths" about each. A positive awareness is created in each and every employee at the firm. The contact also scored points with everyone as he arranged the entertainment, either formally or informally.

The power of the business lunch can never be undersold. Taking your main contacts out to eat and possibly their superiors has been a reliable standard for years. The business relationship becomes stronger, and their personal time is not affected. The lunch can be a simple thank-you for all of their business, or may also entail an effort to gain more business. Again, find the right balance in how much small talk should take place, and how much straight business. The thank-you lunch should be light-hearted and fun. This is a good time to bring your personality to the table, but always remember, stay professional!

The more formal customer outing will create a lasting memory for the customer. Golf outings have been done in this country dating back to the early 20th century. The customer and you participating in something you both enjoy is a win/win. The biggest barrier to these outings is time. Do you and your customer have time for this? If the event is interesting enough to them, they may be willing to go on the weekend. Either way, treating the customer right in a positive atmosphere is the proper approach. Make them feel like a king or queen for a day!

Chapter 7

Grow the Business

The second most important aspect of the Account Executive's duties after retaining the base is to grow the business. This can be done in two ways:

1.) Gain incremental business from current accounts

2.) Close on new accounts

Either one is going to move your numbers in the right direction.

Gaining incremental business from current accounts may come down to the relationship you have established with your customer, and the quality of the product/service already provided. If a strong relationship has been established, the trust factor should be inherent. The greater the trust, the greater chance your customer will order more of your product, or be open to buying other products he usually has gotten from other suppliers. The maxim "Don't put all your eggs in one basket" is prevalent in the business world today. A vendor could close down, downsize, merge with another, or discontinue a product line. The customer does not want to be left without a supplier and have to look for another in a panic. This is a legitimate practice. However, the value of your relationship with the customer trumps that. You know your products, and only want to provide your customer with a quality product or service that will help them grow. They should want the best vendor alliance possible. Where else are they going to find an Account Executive who will look out for them like you do, and have a sincere interest in helping their business instead of just making a close? Where else are they going to find an Account Executive who will be there in a pinch if the regular customer service channels do not satisfy them when they need assistance?

Remember, your relationship with the customer and the service you provide have to be considered as part of the product you're selling. You may have a very good product, but the extra value added that you personally bring to the table makes it outstanding!

Closing on new accounts does not have the benefit of an established relationship, so turn the situation around! Relationships can seem more exciting in the beginning so utilize that perception to your advantage. First impressions are still huge. Maintain a sense of excitement and positive attitude on every call. Produce such a positive atmosphere the prospect actually looks forward to seeing you. Stick to the sales cycle task at hand, and carefully eye drop in other conversations to interest the prospect, staying professional all the while. A stronger relationship is being created with every sales call. At times the close cannot occur until a full professional relationship is established. These are longer closes, and usually are with larger accounts. Persistence, patience, and utilizing the sales cycle method given to you in training can get you there. The close may happen when two things take place:

I.) The prospect believes the product and service with its features can help him or his firm

2.) Trust has formed between you and the prospect

Don't be afraid to show an outside proof source documenting the superiority of your product. Keep a list of current customers who don't mind getting a call and giving their recommendation. I'm amazed by how many prospects actually call to get a current customer's point of view. This really hits home when your current customer uses the same product or service as the prospect, and can provide reasons for switching. Prospects may believe the product or service and its features will help their firms when they understand how the products have helped others:

a. Save their companies time

b. Save their companies money

c. Help provide better service to their customers

Service, money, and time have to be the three biggest buying motivators in today's age.

PCs were supposed to free up time to all employees, but what was not taken into account was that expectations in the business world grew exponentially. Streamlining any current process in a company is always welcome. Freeing up time for employees to tackle other duties is also welcome, and helping your prospects stand out amongst their competition is more than welcome!

Chapter 8

Keep it Simple

Computers have already left their mark on the business world and changed it forever. Corporate workloads and expectations are high. Your customers are experiencing this as well.

The one thing I see Corporate America starving for is simplicity. The business world somehow attained the perception that if it is not complicated, it may not be good enough. My experience has taught me simplicity is better in most cases.

To run your territory efficiently, what are some of the bullet points you want to accomplish?

— Effective time management
— Order in your daily routine
— Flexibility in this routine
— A handle on your customer base
— Pursuit of the Prospects

Time is the most precious resource of a Sales Professional. Every customer can be considered your boss as they are behind your compensation. Customer expectations can be demanding at times, and may require you to perform a task in the middle of the day. Remember, educating the customer after the close may prevent most of these tasks coming to you as the customer will be empowered and know how to solve the issue without your involvement. Also remember, getting your fingernails dirty may be necessary to keep the customer satisfied.

Keep things simple, and expect the unexpected. Lay out your daily planner so you can pursue the biggest bang for your buck. Calling on a large base account in the same geographic area and time span as a large prospect is a good way to start. Allowing extra time later in the day to cold call or use for admin is good because if necessary this time can be directed toward customer emergencies instead. Giving regular attention to your base and allowing enough time to pursue prospects until they become part of your base is a simple but winning approach. This approach will help accomplish the two main goals of a sales professional discussed earlier (maintaining your base and gaining new business).

Counter the corporate expectations levied on you by your own firm with simplicity. In other words, bring simplicity into any tasks that are under your control. My fellow Account Executives were utilizing a complicated tool that outlined their calls one month ahead. I developed one that was much simpler and was easier to read and use while on the road. After getting an ok from my manager, she allowed me to use this for one month. What was the result? I had the best call compliance in the group. Don't be afraid to be creative and try something new as long as it does not go against your company policy.

Introduce simplicity into your customer calls. Computers can now bring graphs and charts into customer presentations with relative ease, but make sure your customers are really looking for this data. It may add flare, but if the customer sees it as too flashy or as useless data he may be turned off. The "to the point" approach in presentations I found to work well, as customers can be overcome with data so easily in today's age. Presenting the nuts and bolts of your product, how it will help them, and any other value added can do the trick.

Introduce simplicity to your firm by channeling suggestions up the chain. No one knows your job as well as you after doing it over time. You may notice how some procedures can be simplified and improved, so don't be afraid to pass these suggestions on. Respectful memos to your manager documenting good ideas should be welcomed. There may be some employees in higher positions who have developed these procedures originally and will take the suggestions the wrong way, so present to your direct manager and let him/her forward in the proper venue if an idea has enough merit. A good corporation should thank you for any suggestions to improve their own routines.

Chapter 9

Seniors, help the Juniors

There is a need in the business and sales worlds for people who don't officially have a Manager Title to take on a leadership role. How many times in battle will the troops, including lieutenants and junior officers, follow the Sergeant who is on his third tour of duty? He has the experience and always finds a way to make it through when the heat is on.

In almost every work group there is an employee who has found his niche, and may have passed on promotions over the years. Anyone who has been in sales with the same company over five years may fit into this category. This sales professional is still challenged by the job, feels the rush, and does not necessarily have the desire to go into management. This employee is usually looked up to by other sales professionals as he has found a way to survive and succeed. This employee consistently meets and surpasses the "what have you done for me lately" challenge.

Whether these people like it or not, they do have a leadership role, especially with new hires. New hires are drawn to these people because they want to know how these veteran employees have found success. What do they do differently? How do they act in front of customers? The veteran sales professional is almost like a professional athlete. Whether they like it or not, professional athletes are role models. Kids do look up to them, and these men and woman are often considered heroes in the eyes of the children watching them. It is a big responsibility.

Here are some good rules to go by for Veteran Sales Professionals:

a. Maintain the "Stay Professional" approach with your coworkers

b. Mentor the new hires

c. Treat the Manager in your group with respect

d. Remember you're part of a team

Just as a Manager is always projecting to others in the work group, so is the Veteran Sale Professional. Always keep this in mind, and handle yourself professionally. You will play a big part in setting the tone for your work group. You are the one who has performed this job the longest. You are the one who has made it through the rough times, so respect is usually given to you. Use this circumstance and help bring a positive work atmosphere to the team. Always be positive, even through challenging times for the company. If you have a good sense of humor, use it at the right time.

Take time to mentor the new hires in your group. You may do this voluntarily or your manager may ask you to do it, but either way it is a great opportunity to help other sales professionals find their way. One-on-one sit-downs, joint rides, and making yourself available to answer their questions over the phone mean a lot to them. Just as you do with your customers during and after the close, educate them so self-sufficiency becomes a part of their day, and they can approach their jobs with new confidence to reach every higher performance levels. They will learn just from watching you in action with your customers. They will notice the rapport you have built up with them, and the balance of strictly business and small talk utilized. They will take great interest in how you handle yourself with prospects or cold calls, and may even interject themselves at the right moment. Always give positive feedback and build them up. Go with them on some of their customer calls to observe them in action. Interject at the right time, and then give constructive feedback after the call, leading with what they did right. These actions and gestures help build a stronger sales professional, team, and company. It is also a paradox, as it comes back to you in many different ways.

It is even more important that Veteran Employees treat their managers with respect. They usually know this as they have been with the company longer and would not have survived with a disrespectful attitude. Sometimes the manager may be a lot newer to the company than the veteran. It is easy for veterans to ask, how can this new person manage me? Don't fall into that trap. Rather, assume that this manager may bring a fresh perspective to the work group. Maybe some of the new ideas brought to the table will be a shot in the arm for everyone. When they feel your support, they should end up doing a better job. Besides, they will informally learn from you as well.

Sales is a performance-based position. Your percent-to-goal, close ratios, etc. are judged heavily. The data is measurable. Everyone goes through dry periods, and keeping a positive mental attitude in the work group during these periods will be an example for everyone. When employees see you're not shaken, you keep trying, and eventually rise to the top of your game again, they learn how to persevere in all circumstances. The Veteran Sales Professional always finds a way to contribute, even when his own territory has run dry. Help your manager, help the team, it may come back to you tenfold. You are the sergeant on the battle field, so meet the challenge of this role. The last of Three Books is all about the management role for those who officially have the title. It can also help the veterans in their unofficial role.

Book III

The Handbook of Management
for Better Business

Roger Reynold

Table of Contents

Book III – The Handbook of Management for Better Business

Dedication 107

Introduction 109

Chapter 1) Attributes of Successful Managers 111

Chapter 2) Building the Manager Employee Relationship.... 115

Chapter 3) Management Integrity 119

Chapter 4) Service Your Employees 123

Chapter 5) Coach and Trainer 127

Chapter 6) The Natural Manager &

       the Called to Management 131

Chapter 7) Managing a Labor Intensive Work Force 135

Chapter 8) Managing the Sales Professional 139

Chapter 9) Managing the Manager 143

Chapter 10) Setting the Course...147

Chapter 11) Notes to Management..151

Dedication

This book is dedicated to all of those in management who realize their employees are their companies' most important resource.

Introduction to Book Three

This last Handbook is designed to awaken the Manager within you. It should elevate your leadership skill set, and bring new dimensions to your management style.

People of today are searching for true leaders in all vocations including sports, politics, and business. People that mean what they say, and are looking out for the people they manage. Society wants to know the people they have elected have their best interests at heart, instead of a self-serving agenda. Employees want to see upper management in a corporation feel they are in the same boat as their employees during challenging times and do everything they can to make their situation better through competent plans and fair decisions.

This book will examine the aspects of management and help the first level management, middle management, and upper management leaders.

Chapter 1

Attributes of Successful Managers

Every Company has some Managers who stand out among peers and employees. These leaders have good reputations and people consider themselves fortunate to work for them. Their goals and challenges are usually achieved and the work groups are productive. What are some of the common characteristics that differentiate these managers?

1.) People Oriented

2.) Respect for Subordinates

3.) Fair and Balanced

4.) Positive Approach

5.) Hard to Rattle

Just as the successful Sales Professional gets in touch with and improves the People Person within him, so must the successful Manager. The successful manager looks forward to people interaction. He recognizes any of his own personal shortcomings that can work against a positive approach to management such as selfishness, jealousy, favoritism, and over-ambition. The manager will work on removing these traits from the management style and in doing so improve his or her professional relationship with the employees.

Effective Managers recognize all employees to some extent are a fragile broken people. They recognize the existence of human flaws, but know people can still accomplish amazing things with the right direction and motivation. The effective Manager treats all employees with equal respect.

Managers who can maintain a positive mental attitude, even under the most negative circumstances, should always out on top. This is demonstrated in all kinds of situations. When an employee acts out or makes continual mistakes, the manager will talk to the employee in private, out of coworker earshot. The Manager will treat the job performance as the problem, and never the employee. (Slowikowski, 1988)

What is needed for the job performance to improve? Does the employee understand the task at hand or is more coaching needed? Is there a disregard for the company directive and if so what is causing this disregard? In the end, the employee will need to change the behavior to meet company expectations. Verbal warnings, writing up the employee, and other punitive actions can always be taken, but the effective manager will first try to understand where the employee is coming from, and improve the chances for the employee to change before anything approaching termination is enacted. Naturally, some behavior, such as violence, cannot be tolerated.

"Managers need to remember they project behavior to their employees. Be sure your behavior is positive." (Slowikowski, 2010)

Whenever they walk into the same room, employees know these people have a different status than other coworkers as they give reviews, delegate tasks, and can help promote or discipline employees. Their actions are magnified because of their position and so they must lead by example. Managers need to remain calm and positive when challenges from above are placed on the work group. How will the work group respond if the leader says the company gave us too much work and too little time to accomplish it? I doubt the team will respond with a can-do attitude.

It is easy for managers to like some employees more than others. This is where the manager must flex her fairness muscles and treat all employees with professional respect and courtesy. How will it look to others if the manager is seen continually making small talk with the same employee? Couldn't some think that person may get a better review or have to do less work? Perceptions are important, and fairness is imperative to keep everyone together as part of one productive team. Equal time given to all employees, positive language used with all employees, and professional courtesy to all will go much farther than singling out a few.

Chapter 2

Building the Manager Employee Relationship

Just as sales professionals strive to build positive relationships with all of their customers, so should the successful manager. Work group employees comprise the manager's internal customers. The sales professional needs external customers to buy a product or service in order to be successful. The manager needs employees (internal customers) to be productive in their tasks in order to be successful.

Managers can take the "my way or the highway" approach and results can be obtained from this. A step further down this road is creating an atmosphere of fear where employees are afraid of getting written up or worse on a daily basis. Usually, these approaches do not heed the results of a positive people approach and are short lived, so PUT FEAR TO THE REAR!

The supervisor can always write up a person if needed, as this is part of the job description. However, if the supervisor has to put this out there often in order for the work group to be productive, things should be reexamined. Remember the Attributes of Successful Managers in the previous chapter? This is a great start to building a positive professional relationship with employees.

Further guidelines for building strong relationships in management are:

1.) Be a good listener

2.) Work outside the box when needed

3.) Know your employees within professional boundaries

4.) Build a positive atmosphere

5.) Build a productive atmosphere

Good managers always listen to their employees. Feedback in reviews, employees' comments concerning new challenges and even subtle body language give an excellent barometer of the individual and work group as a whole. Direct and indirect signals such as these will help shape the leader's approach on a daily basis. Are the employees frustrated? Do they need a motivational speech or just need clarification on their position and that of the company?

Employees may also have excellent input concerning the tasks at hand. They do their jobs more often than anyone else. Wouldn't it stand to reason some of them may have ideas to improve a procedure or even develop a new one resulting in more productivity? Good managers should listen to these ideas and channel them up the ladder if appropriate. If the manager can work outside the box and incorporate these changes into the group, he should do so. Watch other work groups follow when the statistics go up! Creativity from the leader is just as important. Managers always look for ways to improve group job performance and remove barriers to their success.

Managers should get to know their employees within professional limits. Are they married, have kids, like dogs? Knowing personal information like this can help in conversations and bring a personal positive approach to the relationship. It is too easy to only concentrate on work and this can come across as cold. Every employee of yours has their own challenges going on at home as well. Better understanding of your employees can allow better management on your part. Remember to keep the manager-employee relationship professional.

Following the above should foster a positive work atmosphere. There is a synergy in the group employees can sense. Positive attitudes, coworkers treating each other with respect, and high energies can be epidemic. Politics and barriers are minimized. It is no wonder groups such as this lead to greater productivity from individuals and as a whole.

Chapter 3

Management Integrity

As mentioned earlier, leaders are always projecting to others whether they want to or not. Subordinates watch them more closely. Leadership by example is a given. Management Integrity is a must! This is not to say you have to strive to put yourself on a pedestal in each employee's eyes. When this is done, odds are you will fall off. Instead, try to be a real person with integrity. Integrity is always a welcome quality. Dictionaries describe it as adhering to moral principles, and sound character. People always search for this in others and when they find it, trust is elevated to a higher level.

Aside from the previous two chapters on managing, how do you demonstrate integrity in the workplace and model sound principles?

1.) Adhere to your own company's code of conduct first.

2.) When you make a promise, make sure it will be backed up.

3.) Mean what you say, say what you mean.

4.) Manage the whole employee

5.) Understand their point of view

6.) Meet the task at hand

Number one is obvious. A manager can't enforce what he doesn't follow.

Learn the company code of ethics along with implementing common sense.

Number two is remembered among your employees. Be careful when promising anything unless you know you can deliver. Don't promise something if management above you will override it. It can weaken your standing in subordinates' eyes. This also leads into number three. Be straight with employees, but utilize tact. Don't make comments with double meanings. Your employees may not hear what you're actually saying. When you're always straight with your employees, they may not like what you're saying, but should always respect where you're coming from.

Managing the whole employee comes with building the relationship. The more you get to know someone's traits, the more you will be able to help build up their strengths and minimize their shortcomings as it affects job performance. For example, you know one of your employees is going through a stressful time with their children, and this may be affecting their tone of voice in customer interactions. A simple story of how stressful your own kids were the other week could help calm the waters. Remind the employee he/she is not alone in facing work challenges, as well as those that are personal. They are all part of life's pageant, as I heard someone once say.

Positive reinforcement for things done right is always welcome. It reminds people they are doing a good job even though their reviews may be months away. A simple pat on the back from the boss goes a long way. Recognizing improvement in substandard areas is even more welcome. The worker knows he or she is on the right path, and will feel a little more secure in their job along with achieving a stronger sense of accomplishment.

There is always another side, and be happy to listen to the employee's. Sometimes this could open your own eyes to a different viewpoint and a plan of action to address it can be made. Sometimes the employee may just be upset in general. Remind him not every part of the job we will like, and that is the time to dig deep in these circumstances and meet the challenge. The job will have to get done, but you appreciate their feedback!

Chapter 4

Service Your Employees

I can't stress enough the importance of managing employees with an attitude of service. Employees are your internal customers, and should be your first concern. Take care of them, and you'll ultimately take care of your company's external customers.

Managers at all levels wear many hats. The manager is the coach, trainer, vocational guide, and boss. What can get lost in the mix however is the idea that managers are the go-to people for employees, a resource for help. How do managers make sure they are managing with an attitude of service? Follow four simple guidelines:

1.) Set the standard

2.) Be available

3.) Remove the barriers

4.) Have their backs

The first day on the job and in your first group meeting, tell everyone the approach you wish to take. Set the standard and relay to them you are there to help each employee do their job. Your goals for the group are productivity, high energy, and a positive atmosphere. I told one of my groups when it gets to the point where you look forward to coming to work, I've done my job.

Many managers may try to follow the four guidelines, but when employees reach out for assistance the manager may not be accessible. Availability is imperative. Especially with new employees, the manager must be available as there will be more barriers in the beginning. Be there as a resource for the employee, address his or her concerns, educate, and this need should diminish over time. Obviously managers cannot always be available to their staff. They have to take conference calls, attend meetings with upper management, or may be helping another employee. Choosing a veteran in the group as a backup is a good plan. This doubles the resource for employees, and sets the course for a future manager.

When the heat is on, it is even more important to have your employees' backs. These are the times they will most remember if you were there for them. It will be a chance to gain their loyalty. When an upset customer wants to speak to a manager, will you be available to take the call? How will you handle the call? Address the customer in a professional manner, apologize if needed, and resolve the issues. Keep the employee in the know. The fact that the customer asked for a manager may have nothing to do with the employee, but educate that employee afterward if you found any shortcomings. Remember, effective managers can enter adverse circumstances and remain positive!

Be supportive of the employee when going out into the field to meet customers face-to-face if your position allows it. By helping the employee improve her relationship with the customer, you are servicing the employee. Any value added you bring to the table is a win for the customer, your employee, and your corporation.

Your work group performance determines your performance. Their cumulative review scores should determine yours. So make sure you are there for them!

Chapter 5

Coach and Trainer

Many firms have formal training for employees but some may not. It may be up to the Manager to train all of the employees at some corporations. It is definitely up to the manager to coach in real time after they get out of class, if there is one.

Depending on the size of the firm and scope of the job, formal training classes may be available. If the Manager trains employees in a class, he can tap into his job related experience. He may also have taken a class in how to train. The Manager formally training his own employees can be a huge advantage to the company. He not only teaches the mechanical fundamentals of the position, but can also present real world scenarios and what to do about them. The Supervisor may actually be able to steer the course to a place where employees will be ready for the reality of the job sooner, as opposed to strictly adhering to teachings that that can be based solely on theory. Either way, the leader will be more in control during this time, and should have the employee in a good spot by course end.

The Manager may have to formally train the employee outside of a class setting, and conduct the training while on the job. It is important in these situations that a gradual step-by-step process be implemented. Meet with the employee first, be positive and say how glad you are she's on board!

Make sure all of the human resource tasks are completed, and fill her in on the full scope of where she can find the tools or areas she needs in the building or share with her the proper procedures to follow outside of her main duties.

Any easy-to-use written guide on the position would be most welcome by the employee. A quick resource they can go to for help on their own will empower the employee even more at an early stage. Ease the employee into the position, utilizing side-by-sides or joint rides if they go out into the field. Have her actually watch you do the job in real time, stressing what you did right, and could possibly have done better. This is an important time because the employee will see you in action, and gain confidence in you from your job performance. Side-by-sides with veteran employees can be the next step, and finally the employee gets to solo.

The Manager may not be in formal teaching roles as in the above cases, but he may have to coach after the employee solos. Coaching is more flexible than formal training, and not as prearranged. These will be real world job scenarios the Manager will be helping the employee through. The smart manager will let the new employee do the job, always keeping in mind he is just starting out. Observe the job performance and present feedback in a positive way. New employees can feel very vulnerable, so always keep this in mind when presenting feedback. Stress everything done right, and the other areas present as learning opportunities. Any new positive twists they bring to the job because of their individual personalities should be noted as well.

Coaching is the continual duty of the manager. Employees who have done the job for quite a while may start to form bad habits or develop unwelcome shortcuts. These need to be called out by the Manager as he steers them back to proper procedures. Changed habits bring changed outcomes. The longer an employee stays with a company, the more he may think he should not be coached. The good employee probably needs less coaching for sure, but the good manager can always try to bring something fresh to the table to keep him interested.

The Coaching Role will also entail watching over intangibles, namely morale and motivation. These are huge for the effective manager. How many times have sporting teams performed poorly first half, and then turned things around second half because of locker room pep talks? Job tasks and duties performed over time can become dull. The challenge facing veteran employees may be to remain positive and keep performance at high levels even though they have learned all the necessary skill sets. Their attitudes can easily spread to other group members as they are looked up to by others. Make sure the veterans know they are leaders and you need their help in maintaining a positive work atmosphere!

There may be times when individuals must be addressed because of sub standard performance, or perhaps you even need to coach the group as a whole. Brow beating can get short term results, but over time this will add to a negative atmosphere, which sucks up energy like a black hole. The result is group productivity never reaches its full potential. A better way to handle this situation is to address the individual or group with energy. Sub standard performance usually occurs because of a lack of energy or motivation to do the right thing. So, energize the group! Let them feel the enthusiasm in your speech. Tone of voice, choice of words, and body language will all come into play. Show them you are going to a good place, and they should want to follow. You may have to empathize and call them out at the same time, but in the end they should follow your lead.

Chapter 6

The Natural Manager and the Called to Management

I have seen two kinds of Managers in the business world. Those who are natural leaders and those who developed their leadership skills over time and actually felt they were called to it later in their careers. Both types can be very effective managers.

Natural leaders are usually performing at an early age. They instigate the baseball game down the street, or movie outing with friends. They can handle responsibility and the role of decision-maker. People look to them for direction. Common characteristics of "Natural Managers" are:

- Charisma
- Evoke trust
- Confidence
- High Energy
- Good organization skills

Natural Managers can have an outgoing personality. They can grow relationships fairly easily, and are concerned about other people's feelings. They have a positive energy and can be fun to be around outside of the office. Many may have a stronger serious side and need to feel productive most of the time, but this is all channeled in positive ways at work. Natural Managers love their work as it totally fits in with their personality make-up. A management position in an industry they have an interest in results in <u>career passion</u>.

Managers who manage in negative ways can always be found, but those who evoke loyalty from their employees and higher productivity are the Natural Managers who channel their talents toward people-oriented methods. Work groups under these leaders usually have a lower turnover. The experience may be so good an employee will think twice before wanting to move up and out, but effective managers always support career progression, and help to realize true potential in those under them.

Some of the most notable leaders in our country's history did not want the leadership role at all, but despite that, saw a need for it. Some of our past Presidents did not want to run, but they saw a need for a good leader in our country and felt they would make a positive impact. They were willing to trade off privacy in order to help US citizens.

When someone likes the lifestyle they have and only considers a leadership role because they know they can make a positive difference, these people can turn into extraordinary leaders. Personal agendas are not on the table, but rather the sheer desire to help others and improve established formats. They are usually strong people because they are not intimidated by the fear of losing their positions. They know they are only doing this to make a positive impact on the work group or corporation. There can be a very strong momentum behind these leaders that usually results in positive change, and reinforcement of good policy.

I think everyone of good character will ultimately find themselves in a leadership role at some point in their lives. Mother, Father, big brother or sister, it will happen in some way at some point. During a time of crisis an individual can reach inside herself and can take charge, a side of her no one may have seen before. The internal leader comes out at the right time, in order to do the right thing. So, be a good leader on and off the court whenever necessary.

Chapter 7

Managing a Labor Intensive Work Force

Fundamentals of effective management outlined in this book lay a foundation for a positive leadership style applicable to all management positions. Whether you manage a factory, customer service department, or sales force, these principles should be applied. Can there be differences in management styles depending on what work groups you are leading? The answer is yes. Just as individuals in a work group may need individual approaches, so may work groups as a whole. The demands on different jobs may vary.

Duties of labor intensive jobs can be quite different. The assembly line worker may do a repetitive task. The customer service representative may talk to 200 customers a day, but no two calls are exactly alike. Stress can occur in each of these careers, but there are differences.

Managers must first put themselves in the shoes of those they manage. The best managers in these fields are usually those that originally did the job. Employees know their leader has been through the same challenges, and has an understanding of where they're coming from. His comments are usually well accepted. Promotion from within is welcome as it usually ensures an understanding leader and gives employees something to shoot for in career progression. Managing the same work group however can be difficult as those who were once your coworkers are now your subordinates. The employees could have difficulty with your role change, but this can be overcome.

One-on-ones and group meetings provide time for heart-to-hearts and are good ways to start. Accentuate that you obviously know where everyone is coming from. Explain the new position you're in of having to enforce company policy, and at the same time support your employees. Make sure they realize you're an advocate of both!

Managers coming from outside the Company can be effective as well, especially if they worked in a similar industry. Your first meeting can entail a synopsis of your experiences so the employees will be able to relate to your history. By the end of the meeting, make sure they know you've been there. Following the principles outlined earlier of relationship building and the other productive efforts can help ensure your success.

Managers coming from different departments or companies in different industries may have steeper hills to climb. These people may not be able to tell stories of similar job experience. Their first group meetings can vary from the above. The manager needs to stress he is there to help them, and possibly mention how well groups have performed under his leadership. Follow all of the management principles, and also make time every week to perform the same duties as do those you're managing. Respecting the employees and what the employees do will earn their dedication over time.

Different work groups have different needs. Those working on the assembly line do not have customer contact, so blowing off steam from time to time will not hurt any customer relationship. The employee may even be able to do this while still working as long as others are not adversely affected. Customer Service Representatives frustration level may need to be monitored more closely by the Manager. A worsening attitude may show in their calls and how the customer is treated. You don't want the customer service representative to use a customer as a valve release. These reps may have to sign off in these circumstances and leave the room for a bit. Better to take less customer calls than to damage the company's relationship with those customers.

In the end, employees want a strong leader in the Manager Seat who finds the right balance of employee interaction. Someone who remains positive and the employees can count on when the heat is on. Someone who can funnel the directives from upper management down to them in an attainable way. Someone who won't come across as above them, but rather as one who is there to serve and remove the barriers to productivity. Work groups who are placed in this environment can light it up!

Chapter 8

Managing the Sales Professional

How do you manage a group of Type-A personalities? Sales Management can be considered a different breed of supervision. The Manager's performance is totally dependent on the performance quotient of the sales team. The Manager lives or dies by the district numbers. Let us not forget the proverbial "What have you done for me lately," which always seems to be looming.

Unlike the stress that comes from repetitive tasks in the assembly line or the multiple wants of customers that surface in a customer service center, sales has a different kind of tension. It can be prevalent when the percent-to-goal and closes are down, or more subtle when the numbers are sufficient but worries exist over some large accounts in danger. This stress can be taken home very easily and "sleepless nights" can occur until the sales representative and manager are confident the account is satisfied. Remember, the Account Executive may be responsible for forty accounts or more, but the Sales Manager is responsible for these times seven team members. What do the Account Executives look for in their Manager?

1.) A proven track record of sales experience and performance

2.) Availability to interface with larger accounts

3.) Support during times of customer dilemmas

4.) Value added brought to the Sales Professional and Customer

5.) Package Upper Management Directives as user friendly

The Sales Manager that can come through on the above five points is well on his way to a performing work group. The Sales Manager should be considered a secret weapon that can be sprung on larger prospects or accounts in jeopardy when needed. Customers will be impressed by a District Manager visit. You may see customers even wear a tie and suit especially for the occasion.

In addition to the above, the Sales Manager must be flexible and allow the Sales Professionals to manage their territories. At times when numbers are down the Manager may start to enforce more directives, which is understandable. Maybe the group needs a little wake-up call to get them selling again. However, the Manager should guard against handcuffing the sales force so they are not free to incorporate the principles outlined in Book II.

So how does the Sales Manager begin interfacing? First, the Manager must support the internal customers (i.e. the Sales Professionals) through the above bullet points. Meet with each Account Executive, develop that relationship, and commit to side-by-sides and joint rides. Accentuate their positives and coach the areas needing improvement. Make them excited about selling again! Wake up the Sales Professionals who are resting on their laurels. Sooner or later these Account Executives will need to sell again, regardless of how large accounts were closed on less than a year ago.

Second, interface with the needed customers. The Sales Manager will not be able to visit every account, so explain to the Account Executive that you are there for them, but are also a limited resource. You are there to solidify any base accounts in danger, reinforce the larger accounts, and help close with prospects. Bring value added to these joint calls, so the customer and Sales Professional are glad you came. Don't rain on your AE's parade, but show the customer you value their business and are there to improve their company performance wherever possible. This reinforces the partnership approach and a mutual beneficial relationship!

Keeping time consuming barriers to a minimum is imperative for the Sales Manager. Time is one of the most precious resources for the Sales Professional. Corporations may levy a number of administrative tasks on these professionals, which are needed but can be time consuming. Help the employee get into good habits and address tasks daily so they are not mounting up at the end of the week, which diminishes selling time and increases frustration. Develop new out-of-the-box methods for your crew to use when tackling administrative tasks. Empower your Account Executives as much as you can. When a sales professional continually does the right thing, the numbers should follow.

Finally, the Sales Manager should notice the potential in every employee. The Sales Professional may feel very vulnerable much of the time. Competition may be huge in the marketplace, and accomplished Sales Professionals don't take anything for granted. Top performers may go through down times from overselling the territories, or lose a large account through no fault of their own. Stand behind these employees, and it will probably reward you at a later time. Help the new hires get into the selling groove. If they care about their jobs, they should develop attitudes of patience and persistence until the first big close is obtained. When mistakes are made, help the sales person learn from the experience and teach him or her to dig deep for the future. Motivate the sales force, move the numbers. Accentuate the positive, coach past the negative. Seek and remove the barriers, and the sales force can be self sustaining.

The Sales Force drives Corporate Revenue. When the economy is down, the Corporation turns to Sales even more. How more important will the Sales Leadership be during these trying times?

Chapter 9

Managing the Manager

Company Presidents, Vice-Presidents, and Directors all direct those in management. The higher up the chain, the more responsible they are for the overall picture of the Firm. Corporate planning, setting directives, establishing goals, and formatting time tables all come into play with the more promotions received. What are some of the basics all of these "Managers" have in common? They are all a leader's leader!

The Manager's Manager usually stood out amongst her peers when she was at a straight Management Level. Her work group usually had better statistics and seemed more motivated. She was the one other managers came to for advice. When the heat was on, her group always found a way to make it happen and meet the goals. What better person to promote so her business philosophy and way of doing things can be spread to other managers and groups?

Effective Directors should be abundant in "the attributes"; with respect for others, being people-oriented, fair and balanced. Management integrity is a given and training aptitude is quite high. An effective Director believes the company she works for offers a valuable product or service. Career passion is a common trait, as dedication and going the extra mile usually got her where she is. The more enthusiasm in management, the more subordinates will believe what they do has value. High energy levels can be contagious to all employees.

We discussed how managers continually project to others when they come into a room, Directors and above project even more. All of the employees know this is their boss's boss speaking and want to make and maintain a good impression. Directors' words will be hung on to just a little longer. Attention levels will be just a bit higher. So, Directors need to be good speakers. Many an orator may make valuable points, but if the speech comes across as flat and monotone the importance of the words may be lost. A higher confidence level should always be presented, even if the Director is unsure about the new directives from above. New procedures and courses of action may need to be "sold" to the employees. They will be looking at the Director for a belief in these changes. The reaction to these changes if the Director is unsure could be accompanied by a grudge-laden attitude.

A Good Director may need to fight for the "little guy." He will delve deep into his past and remember what the job entailed on the front lines. He may remember how he would try to implement change for everyone if he ever got to a higher decision-making level. This was a subconscious commitment made and now that he has the owner or President's ear it should be followed up. He may find the opportunity to present a proposal that may increase productivity and company morale! It is not surprising that in many cases the two go hand in hand.

Good Directors respect the knowledge base and experiences of all the managers under their supervision. These people usually became proficient in their duties to reach their career levels. Some of these managers may feel they have found their niche specializing in managing a specific team and do not want to go any higher. Good Directors will look forward to a diverse team of managers and realize all of the Managers' unique personalities can bring a variety of positive management styles to the work force. They will guide all of the managers in eliminating any non productive and negative management traits, and strengthen their positive ones. When this is done, imagine what this team of managers can accomplish?

Chapter 10

Setting the Course

Setting the course should be done to some degree at all management levels. Front Line and Middle Management will be most influential in setting the tone for their work groups and streamlining procedures wherever possible. The Director can actually influence policies and suggest formal changes. Steering the overall course of the Corporation is usually reserved for Vice-Presidents and above. Their input and ideas will all steer where the Corporation is going.

To make effective decisions at this level, what considerations should those in charge take into account?

1.) Examine what customers like about the current product or services

2.) Determine what they will want and need in the future

3.) Grow the company's reputation as a good place to work

4.) Achieve the monetary goals necessary for the well being of the Corporation and stock holders (if any).

Points one through four are a simplistic way of determining a Corporate Path, but remember, simplicity can be a good thing. Points one through four can only be achieved when feedback is obtained from customers and employees interfacing with them. Employees dealing directly with ultimate customers have the highest degree of the customer relationship. The Corporate/Customer Mutual Beneficial Relationship can be found right there in every customer interface and upper management needs to examine these to learn the customers' wants, needs, and concerns. Monitoring sessions and side-by-sides between upper management and employees dealing directly with customers may reveal all of these. Good relationships between managers and employees along with clear communication paths can as well. Too many times fear in Corporate America may prevent employees from channeling or presenting viable ideas upward. As stated before, put Fear to the Rear! The history of this country is filled with individuals and groups putting fresh ideas into action. Make sure your Corporation has the same openness to innovative concepts, as they may be necessary for its survival down the road.

I am a big believer in simplicity as mentioned earlier in the Three Books. The accelerated pace Corporate America faces brought about by computer implementation and company expectations is huge. Employees and consumers are looking for ideas that will bring order to their lives and free up time. I remember my father had more time to complete projects and make sure they were done correctly in his younger years. When computers came into their own, my dad was expected to do twice and three times the work in the same amount of time, with the same quality. At times, the time saving aspects of computers did not keep up with work expectations. He had to simplify his own habits and procedures to adapt.

I know of a gentleman who is very good with Excel spreadsheets. He loved to outline his ideas and concerns in Excel. He had a knack for putting complicated procedures into a user-friendly, easy-to-understand spreadsheet. I actually forwarded some examples to coworkers who were very impressed. My friend took this as a huge compliment. He never thought he was very technical because of his need to simplify, but I told him this is needed in today's age. The ability to take intricate business concepts, ideas, procedures, and present them in a user friendly format is priceless!

Finally, the ship should always be steered with good intentions and avoid the abyss of personal agendas. Good business relationships and good productivity usually got upper management where they are today, so no one in this group should want to jeopardize that. Lead your employees to higher levels of customer relationships. Make sure your company is better off with your decisions than without them. The responsibilities and consequences are high, and so are the rewards. Putting monetary gains aside, what greater satisfaction is there than when officers see their companies prosper from their efforts and decisions? What is more uplifting than seeing higher satisfaction among employees and customers, which bring about stronger internal and external customer relationships? Companies building on these principles can endure and become beacons of light in the business world.

Light up the path.

Chapter 11

Notes to Management

Many notes to management have been discussed in this book. Let us review them:

Note to management – Make sure everyone at the company realizes the importance of what they do, and how it eventually affects the customer.

Note to management – Training employees on your companies' products should be fully covered in training. Also, cyclical instruction throughout the year on current and new products is highly recommended.

Note to management – Recognize employees who have done their job for some time and done it well. Awards and promotions within a department give the employee something to strive for, and increases morale.

Note to management – Recognize the need for MPUB, (Mentally Prepare, Pace Yourself, Utilize Breaks, and have a Back-Up Plan: From Book I Chapter 4). You may have different suggestions for each individual to help them deal with the day-to-day stress of their duties.

Note to management – Make sure every employee understands they are truly "representing" their entire company, in their duties, just as sales professionals do out in the field.. Their actions can affect the bottom line as much as revenue generating departments.

Note to management – Keep procedures for customers as simple as possible such as phone menus. Menus which are too intricate and require too many "punches" can create frustration on the part of the customer.

Note to management – Always keep the door open to listening to your employees concerning customer concerns, issues, and patterns. Keep your door open to upper management as well to channel this information up.

Note to Retail Management – Please keep communication open between you and your retail personnel. Listen to their feedback regarding customer flow and "hot times" when extra help or back-up may be needed.

Note to Management – Added incentives are a good way to increase corporate revenue, and also motivate the work force. A little reimbursement for every Customer Rep who makes a sale or reaches a sales goal can bring a new, positive dimension to the job.

Note to Sales Management – Relay the importance of FEM to your sales force, (Book II, Chapter 3. Follow-up, Educate, Maintain).

Note to Sales Management – The notion that if a person does a good job in customer service, he or she may not do well in sales because they'll be doing more servicing than selling, is being reassessed. Many good customer service agents have later proved themselves in the sales force (myself included). Many CSRs may have a strong desire to sell as their next career challenge. Training to get them more in the selling mode along with their already present FEM mindset may allow them to excel. Keep this in mind during your next set of interviews for an open territory.

All of the above add up to four things: Management taking care of their most important internal customers (their employees), management making their corporation a stronger company, management allowing better service for external customers, and increased sales. Managers who accomplish the aforementioned are certainly performing well in the most important aspects of their job. They are removing barriers hindering employee performance and improving company processes already in place. Managers who can take these steps and keep a positive frame of mind during stressful times are usually very popular, and employees want to work for them. Also, the work productivity of these groups can be high. People-oriented management pays off!

-Afterword I-

What is Success in Business?

Success in the business world has often been measured by reaching a financial goal or the gaining of prosperity. Individuals may measure it as reaching a wanted salary or maintaining a certain lifestyle. A corporation may measure it by stock value, or yearly profits. I contend there is a deeper meaning to this phrase. Let us again "simplify" and look at this term as it applies to Career Success, and Success of a Corporation.

-Career Success

I remember sitting on the couch watching a movie. The movie had a mother and son living together. The mother took in washing to support the family, and there was laundry stacked all over the apartment, and I mean all over the apartment. The son's target was to make a lot of money and deliver his mother from the perceived drudgery. After finally making his goal, he came into the kitchen one day and told her she would not have to take in any more washing. His mother then became discouraged thinking she had to give up her career. (Johnny Dangerously, DVD, 2002)

Now which one of these individuals had career success? One of them went down a shady path in crime. The other still liked what she did, saw the value in it, and supported her family from it.

That is what career success is. When someone recognizes the value in what he does, believes it makes the world a better place, and has an inner peace or satisfaction by doing it. People using their God Given Talents who found themselves usually stand out in whatever they do, be it a Maintenance Engineer, Police Officer, Teacher, or Vice President of a Bank. There is an attitude and energy about them drawn from liking what they do, and being at peace with it.

I have seen a number of people over the years that have found themselves, but don't even realize it. Their goals are always changing, want to always make more money, and so don't recognize the good things they are achieving right now. Others I've noticed actually like what they do, but always feel they aren't doing enough, or aren't using enough of their talents. Maybe these people will do something else later on in the same field and at a more challenging level. These people may also want to try and channel their talents more in their private lives.

Finally, we've all met people who may not like what they do, but feel they are stuck, (i.e., they need to support their family, kids going to college, etc). These individuals need to first take stock in themselves and the situation, and then give themselves some credit! They should ask themselves the following:

1.) Is this honest work?

2.) Does the work have value?

3.) What am I accomplishing from it?

Usually when you ask yourself these three questions, you start to feel better about what you do, and yourself. Many of us ask ourselves from time to time "Maybe I should have done that instead, or what would have happened if I chose another field?" This is totally normal. There's a little uncertainty in all of us, and sometimes this can drive positive change. Deep down if you believe you should be doing something else, it may be a good idea to reach out to others as well as your own faith. You may be surprised however and discover you actually did what you were supposed to do.

Think of the number of careers out there which touch so many lives but don't get a lot of recognition in this life. Substitute Teachers, Junior Sport Referees, and Tour Guides to name a few. These people come into contact with many others on a daily basis. They can make positive or negative impressions on them pending on how they perform their duties. They won't be making the $6,000,000 a year salaries as some of our famed sports athletes do, but they have a lot of human interactions just the same. My good friend Robert currently substitute teaches full time. Kids will come up to me if they realize I know him and tell me about the good things which happened in his class just for that one day. He made a positive impression on them and something he said may have helped steer their lives in the right direction and have long time affects. His sister taught music and she made lasting impressions on her students. Again, very important careers and ironically minimal rewards, but only on the surface!

-Success of a Corporation

To see if a company is "Successful", what should be looked at? Profit is important, as it is necessary for a Corporation to grow and stick around. Should profit be the sole measuring stick however?

Corporations need to realize their two most important aspects are actually:

1.) The product or service they offer

2.) The employees who work for them

Here goes my need to simplify again but points one and two are the most important components of any company. Employees can easily forget the products or services they produce improve society. There is an actual need for what they make, and hence should be proud of what they do. Too many times employees may fall into a rut over the years and just look forward to their weekly paycheck, and the weekend. They forget that what they do has value and helps others.

Companies need to remember that no matter how good their products and services are, they would not happen without their employees. Companies who take stock in their own employees' first instead of quarterly numbers can many times be more successful. These companies usually have a great reputation, instill loyalty from those who work for them, and get positive press from internal and external customers.

After considering all of the above, two good measurements of a successful corporation are:

1.) Does the product or service it produces improve society?

2.) Do employees overall like working for the company?

If the answers to these two questions are yes, the owners and/or stock holders have a Winner on their hands!

-Afterword II-

The Ultimate Customer, Profit, and the Free Market

Just as Corporations should not forget that employees make their goods and services possible, they should also not forget that profit comes from their Consumers or "Ultimate Customers". Corporations which have good employment reputations and produce quality products can draw consumers to purchase them.

The wants and needs of the Ultimate Customers need to be considered then when targeting profits and setting financial goals. A quality product or service fitting the needs of the consumer in any given time should be in demand. How much profit then should be targeted? I contend there are two profit targets:

1.) Healthy Profit

2.) Whatever the free market will bare

Healthy Profit considers the consumer directly. It examines the times the consumer is in and balances what a healthy cost is for the product versus an excessive price. A "healthy product cost" allows the Corporation to sustain itself, grow, and reach future goals. It also provides the consumer with a quality product at a reasonable price.

If the product is in very high demand because of its uniqueness or quality, it can be very easy to charge more and incorporate the "Whatever the Market will Bare" approach. This path needs to be cautioned as another company can come along, copy your product with some minor changes, and then charge lower. Striving toward healthy profit and cost can create a win / win for the Corporation and Consumer and instill a loyal customer following. Always pushing the envelope for maximum profits can eventually price the product off the free market.

The age old free market foundations of Supply and Demand and competition cannot be avoided. Consumers ultimately have the final say in what they will purchase. Corporations that target creating quality products and services, instill positive work environments, and setting healthy costs may become industry front-runners.

-Thank you to the Reader-

Thank you for buying and reading <u>The Three Books of Business</u>. I hope it brought about fresh ideas and approaches to your current position and future career path. I also hope you took the time to read all three of the Handbooks as they are all interrelated. The Manager can find value in reading The Handbook of Service for Good Business and The Handbook of Sales for More Business. The Customer Service Representative will gain insights into where management is coming from in The Handbook of Management for Better Business. Higher understanding gives way to better communication, which results in better innovation. Continue to make your work environment a better place.

Roger Reynold

-References-

Norb Slowikowski; "Developing Leadership Skills" Lecture; William Rainey Harper College; Palatine, Illinois; April 12, 1988

Norb Slowikowski; email to author; January 27, 2010

Steinberg, Norman; Harry Colomby; Jeff Harris; Bernie Kukoff; Johnny Dangerously; DVD; Directed by Amy Heckerling; Beverly Hills, California; 20th Century Fox Home Entertainment; 2002.